Svelte with Test-Driven Development

Advance your skills and write effective automated tests with Vitest, Playwright, and Cucumber.js

Daniel Irvine

BIRMINGHAM—MUMBAI

Svelte with Test-Driven Development

Group Product Manager: Rohit Rajkumar
Publishing Product Manager: Bhavya Rao
Content Development Editor: Abhishek Jadhav
Technical Editor: Simran Ali
Copy Editor: Safis Editing
Project Coordinator: Sonam Pandey
Proofreader: Safis Editing
Indexer: Rekha Nair
Production Designer: Jyoti Chauhan
Marketing Coordinator: Nivedita Pandey

First published: July 2023

Production reference: 1060623

Published by Packt Publishing Ltd.
Livery Place
35 Livery Street
Birmingham
B3 2PB, UK.

ISBN 978-1-83763-833-8

www.packtpub.com

Contributors

About the author

Daniel Irvine is a software consultant based in London. He works with a variety of languages, including C#, Clojure, JavaScript, and Ruby. He's a mentor and coach for developers and runs TDD and XP workshops and courses. When he's not working, he spends time cooking and practicing yoga. He co-founded the Queer Code London meetup and is an active member of the European Software Craft community. He is the author of *Mastering React Test-Driven Development* (Packt), now in its second edition, and *Build Your Own Test Framework* (Apress). He can be contacted through his website: www.danielirvine.com.

I want to thank my developer friends and colleagues at Mindful Chef, in particular Aleksandra Sezer, Brendan Murphy, James Edward-Jones, James Graham, James Teale, Mark McDermid, Tito Molina, and Zack Xu, who all assisted me during the authoring process. The team at Packt have been brilliant, as usual, giving me exactly the support I needed to complete the book. Thanks in particular to Bhavya Rao, Sonam Pandey, and Abhishek Jadhav. I look forward to our next project!

About the reviewer

Aakash Goplani is a JavaScript developer with eight years of rich experience in developing web applications using Angular and Svelte. Aakash is also experienced in developing hybrid mobile applications using Ionic. Apart from web development, Aakash has also worked on content management systems using Oracle WebCenter Sites.

Table of Contents

13

Part 3: Testing SvelteKit Features

14

15

16

Preface

What excites me about Svelte? Its simplicity, elegance, and pragmatic design ethos. Its growing success in the marketplace suggests that other programmers feel the same way too. I'm not surprised by this. When we write software for the JavaScript ecosystem, we have a choice: we can either accept and be consumed by the complexity of its primary constituents (React, Node.js, webpack, Babel, and so on) or we can actively seek out the marginalized products and processes that aim to simplify our work.

It'll be no surprise to you that I place **Test-Driven Development (TDD)** firmly in this second camp. Because without it, what you have is a development workflow that largely consists of chasing bugs and carrying a lot of context in your head. This is always what I think of as the *bad old days*.

When I first started programming as a youngster, I remember the infuriating experience of debugging – writing some code, trying it out, finding bugs, and struggling for hours to figure out where the errors were hidden in my code. It seemed like a natural part of programming: devoting a large portion of my time to debugging. And this carried through into my first job as a C++ desktop application developer. (It wasn't long before I discovered TDD and how it could help me have a simpler, quieter, calmer life.)

Then there's the mental context you need when you plan out a grand design for the next feature you're about to implement. You have to know where you're at, what you've done, and what's next, and do your best to not stray from the path. That's hard when you're being derailed by debugging and other distractions.

Sure, you can write a to-do list or keep a diary, but why not write some automated tests instead? They not only remind you where you're at but they check for bugs, too.

That is essentially the idea behind TDD.

And if you like Svelte because it simplifies your life and makes you feel like you're swimming rather than wading through mud, I think you'll also like TDD. This book shows you the how and why of Svelte with TDD. I hope you enjoy it. Thanks for reading!

Who this book is for

If you're a Svelte programmer, this book is for you. I aim to show you how TDD can improve your work. If you're already knowledgeable about TDD, I hope there's still a lot you can learn from comparing your own process with mine.

If you don't already know Svelte, but you're familiar with any modern frontend framework such as React, you should be able to follow along and pick things up as you go. TDD is a wonderful platform for explaining new technologies, and it's entirely plausible that you'll be able to pick up Svelte simply by following this book.

What this book covers

Chapter 1, Setting up for Testing, covers the SvelteKit package and configuring your development environment for effective TDD work with both the Vitest and Playwright test runners.

Chapter 2, Introducing the Red-Green-Refactor Workflow, shows how the basic TDD process works, and discusses why it's useful. It introduces the Vitest test runner for writing unit tests.

Chapter 3, Loading Data into a Route, demonstrates how to load data into a Svelte page component using TDD. It introduces the Playwright test runner for writing end-to-end tests.

Chapter 4, Saving Form Data, shows how to implement a basic HTML form along with its submit action.

Chapter 5, Validating Form Data, adds form validation rules to the form built in *Chapter 4*.

Chapter 6, Editing Form Data, shows how TDD can be used to evolve a system design, by modifying the form to work in edit mode.

Chapter 7, Tidying up Test Suites, switches focus to look at techniques for better testing, starting with a look at how test suites can be kept neat and tidy.

Chapter 8, Creating Matchers to Simplify Tests, explains an advanced technique for managing the complexity of test suites: creating and using expectation matcher functions.

Chapter 9, Extracting Logic Out of the Framework, discusses how you can make your application design more testable by moving logic out of framework-controlled modules.

Chapter 10, Test-Driving API Endpoints, looks at how you can use TDD to implement API calls.

Chapter 11, Replacing Behavior with a Side-By-Side Implementation, shows how TDD is useful even when faced with complex refactoring exercises.

Chapter 12, Using Component Mocks to Clarify Tests, introduces the most complex piece of frontend automated testing: component mocking.

Chapter 13, Adding Cucumber Tests, introduces the Cucumber test framework and shows how it can be applied to a SvelteKit project.

Chapter 14, Testing Authentication, shows an approach to writing both unit and end-to-end tests for authentication libraries.

Chapter 15, Test-Driving Svelte Stores, provides a brief look at how Svelte stores can be effectively tested.

Chapter 16, Test-Driving Service Workers, shows how to write automated tests for service workers, as supported by the SvelteKit framework.

To get the most out of this book

There are two ways to read this book.

The first is to use it as a reference when you are faced with specific testing challenges. Use the index to find what you're after and move to that page.

The second, and the one I'd recommend starting with, is to follow the walk-throughs step by step, building your own code base as you go along. The companion GitHub repository has a directory for each chapter (such as Chapter01) and then, within that, two directories:

- Start, which is the starting point for the chapter; you should start here if you're following along.
- Complete, which contains completed solutions to all the exercises.

You will need to be at least a little proficient with **Git**; a basic understanding of the branch, checkout, clone, commit, diff, and merge commands should be sufficient.

Take a look at the README.md file in the GitHub repository for more information and instructions on working with the code base.

If you are using the digital version of this book, we advise you to type the code yourself or access the code from the book's GitHub repository (a link is available in the next section). Doing so will help you avoid any potential errors related to the copying and pasting of code.

Download the example code files

You can download the example code files for this book from GitHub at https://github.com/PacktPublishing/Svelte-with-Test-Driven-Development. If there's an update to the code, it will be updated in the GitHub repository.

We also have other code bundles from our rich catalog of books and videos available at https://github.com/PacktPublishing/. Check them out!

Download the color images

We also provide a PDF file that has color images of the screenshots and diagrams used in this book. You can download it here: https://packt.link/GD8Lg.

Conventions used

There are a number of text conventions used throughout this book.

`Code in text`: Indicates code words in text, database table names, folder names, filenames, file extensions, pathnames, dummy URLs, user input, and Twitter handles. Here is an example: "We can start with a test that specifies what this `Birthday` component will do with its `name` prop."

A block of code is set as follows:

```
import { describe, it, expect } from 'vitest';
import {
  render,
  screen
} from '@testing-library/svelte';
import Birthday from './Birthday.svelte';
```

When we wish to draw your attention to a particular part of a code block, the relevant lines or items are set in bold:

```
describe('Birthday', () => {
  it('displays the name of the person', () => {
    render(Birthday, { name: 'Hercules' });
  });
});
```

Any command-line input or output is written as follows:

```
mkdir birthdays
cd birthdays
npm create svelte@latest
```

Bold: Indicates a new term, an important word, or words that you see onscreen. For instance, words in menus or dialog boxes appear in **bold**. Here is an example: "The user clicks the **Save** button."

> **Tips or important notes**
> Appear like this.

Get in touch

Feedback from our readers is always welcome.

General feedback: If you have questions about any aspect of this book, email us at customercare@ packtpub.com and mention the book title in the subject of your message.

Errata: Although we have taken every care to ensure the accuracy of our content, mistakes do happen. If you have found a mistake in this book, we would be grateful if you would report this to us. Please visit www.packtpub.com/support/errata and fill in the form.

Piracy: If you come across any illegal copies of our works in any form on the internet, we would be grateful if you would provide us with the location address or website name. Please contact us at copyright@packt.com with a link to the material.

If you are interested in becoming an author: If there is a topic that you have expertise in and you are interested in either writing or contributing to a book, please visit authors.packtpub.com.

Share Your Thoughts

Once you've read *Svelte with Test-Driven Development*, we'd love to hear your thoughts! Scan the QR code below to go straight to the Amazon review page for this book and share your feedback.

https://www.amazon.in/review/create-review/error?asin=1837638330

Your review is important to us and the tech community and will help us make sure we're delivering excellent quality content.

Download a free PDF copy of this book

Thanks for purchasing this book!

Do you like to read on the go but are unable to carry your print books everywhere?

Is your eBook purchase not compatible with the device of your choice?

Don't worry, now with every Packt book you get a DRM-free PDF version of that book at no cost.

Read anywhere, any place, on any device. Search, copy, and paste code from your favorite technical books directly into your application.

The perks don't stop there, you can get exclusive access to discounts, newsletters, and great free content in your inbox daily

Follow these simple steps to get the benefits:

1. Scan the QR code or visit the link below

https://packt.link/free-ebook/9781837638338

2. Submit your proof of purchase
3. That's it! We'll send your free PDF and other benefits to your email directly

Part 1:
Learning the TDD Cycle

The first part introduces the **Test-Driven Development** (TDD) workflow and explains how you can use it to build Svelte applications.

This part has the following chapters:

1

Setting up for Testing

Back when you were a young schoolchild, you probably learned to write by using a pencil on paper. Now that you're older, it's likely you prefer pens. For learners, pencils have a distinct advantage over pens in that mistakes are easy to correct, and when you first start writing out letters and words, you will be making a lot of mistakes. Pencils are also safer for small children – no caps or messy ink to worry about.

But pencils remain a valid writing instrument, and you might still have a personal preference for pencils over pens. The pencil is a perfectly good tool for the job.

Test-Driven Development (TDD) is a tool that can serve you in a similar way. It's a great way to learn and grow as a developer. Many experienced developers prefer it for their day-to-day work over any alternative.

In this chapter, you'll configure a work environment that's designed to help you get the most out of TDD techniques. Since TDD asks you to do a bunch of small repetitive tasks – writing tests, running tests, committing early and often, and switching between test code and application code – it's important that each of those tasks can be done easily and quickly.

It follows that an important personal discipline to cultivate is that of objectively critiquing your development tools. For every tool that you use, ask yourself this: is this tool serving me well? Is it easy and quick to use?

This could be your **Integrated Development Environment** (IDE), your operating system, your source code repository, your note-taking program, your time management utilities, and so on. Anything and everything you use in your day job. Scrutinize your tools. Throw away whatever isn't working for you.

This is a very personal thing and depends a lot on experience and individuality. And your preferences are likely to change over time, too.

I often reach for very plain, simple, keyboard-driven tools that work for me consistently, regardless of the programming language I'm working in, such as the text editor Vim. It doesn't offer any knowledge about the JavaScript programming language or the Svelte framework, but it makes me extremely effective at editing text.

But if you care about learning JavaScript or program design, then you might prefer an IDE that gives you JavaScript auto-complete suggestions and helpful project assistance.

This chapter walks through the setup of a new SvelteKit project and highlights all the individual choices you'll need to make, and the additional extras you'll need in order to practice effective TDD.

It covers the following topics:

- Creating a new SvelteKit project

- Preparing your development environment for frequent test runs

- Configuring support for Svelte component tests

- Optional configuration you may want to try

By the end of the chapter, you'll know how to create a new Svelte project that is ready for test-driven feature building.

Technical requirements

The code for the chapter can be found online at `https://github.com/PacktPublishing/Svelte-with-Test-Driven-Development/tree/main/Chapter01/Start`.

You will need to have a recent version of Node.js installed. See `https://nodejs.org` for instructions on how to install and update Node.js for your platform.

Creating a new SvelteKit project

In this section, you'll use the default method for creating a new SvelteKit project, which uses the npm `create` command. (For reference, you can also check the official documentation at `https://kit.svelte.dev/docs/creating-a-project`.)

The project we are building is called *Birthdays* and the npm package name is `birthdays`. It will be introduced properly in *Chapter 2*, *Introducing the Red-Green-Refactor Workflow*.

> **SvelteKit 1.0**
>
> These instructions were valid at the time of writing, for SvelteKit 1.0. It's likely things will improve in time, so you may find some of the later instructions will become unnecessary or may no longer work. Check the book's GitHub repository for the most up-to-date instructions.

For now, we'll concentrate on the mechanics of building a new project:

1. Start by opening a Terminal window in your usual work location (for me, this is ~/work on my Mac). Then type the following commands:

    ```
    mkdir birthdays
    cd birthdays
    npm create svelte@latest
    ```

    If this is the first Svelte project you've created, you'll be presented with the following message from npm:

    ```
    Need to install the following packages:
      create-svelte@2.1.0
    Ok to proceed? (y)
    ```

2. Answer y to that. You'll see a bunch more questions, which we'll go through individually:

    ```
    create-svelte version 2.1.0

    Welcome to SvelteKit!

    ? Where should we create your project?
    (leave blank to use current directory) >
    ```

3. Since you're already in the birthdays directory, just leave this blank, and hit *Enter*. Next, you'll be asked about which app template you'd like to use:

    ```
    ? Which Svelte app template? > - Use arrow-keys. Return to
    submit.
        SvelteKit demo app
    >   Skeleton project - Barebones scaffolding for your new
    SvelteKit app
        Library skeleton project
    ```

4. Choose Skeleton project. Next, you'll be asked about TypeScript:

    ```
    ? Add type checking with TypeScript? > - Use arrow-keys. Return
    to submit.
        Yes, using JavaScript with JSDoc comments
        Yes, using TypeScript syntax
    >   No
    ```

5. For this question, I've chosen No. That's because this book is about testing techniques, not typing techniques. That's not to say that this book doesn't apply to TypeScript projects – it most certainly does – just that typing is not the topic at hand.

> **If you want to use TypeScript**
>
> If you're a seasoned TypeScript developer, please feel free to choose that option instead. The code samples in the book won't need too much modification except for the additional type definitions, which you'll need to provide.

6. Finally, you'll be asked about extra package dependencies:

    ```
    ? Add ESLint for code linting? > No / Yes
    ? Add Prettier for code formatting? > No / Yes
    ? Add Playwright for browser testing? > No / Yes
        ✔ Add Vitest for unit testing? … No / Yes
    ```

7. Choose Yes as the answer to all these questions. Although we won't mention ESLint in this book, it's always good to have. And we'll need Playwright and Vitest.

    You'll then see a summary of all your choices, followed by a Next steps list:

    ```
    Your project is ready!
    ✔ ESLint
      https://github.com/sveltejs/eslint-plugin-svelte3
    ✔ Prettier
      https://prettier.io/docs/en/options.html
      https://github.com/sveltejs/prettier-plugin-svelte#options
    ✔ Playwright
      https://playwright.dev
    ✔ Vitest
      https://vitest.dev

    Install community-maintained integrations:
      https://github.com/svelte-add/svelte-adders

    Next steps:
      1: npm install (or pnpm install, etc)
      2: git init && git add -A && git commit -m "Initial commit"
    (optional)
      3: npm run dev -- --open
    ```

    We'll perform these next steps but before we do that, we'll run some extra verification steps. It's always good to check your work.

Type npm install into the Terminal and confirm that everything is installed correctly. Then, go ahead and commit your changes. (If you've forked the GitHub repository, you won't need to use the git init command.)

> **Committing early and often**
>
> It's a good idea to be checking in your work very often. While you're learning the TDD approach to testing, it can be helpful to check in after every single test. This might seem like a lot but it will help you backtrack in case you get stuck.

Then, run npm run dev - -open. It should open your web browser and show you a "Welcome to SvelteKit" message.

You can then close the browser and hit *Ctrl + C* in the Terminal to stop the web server.

Next, let's verify the Playwright and Vitest dependencies.

Installing and running Playwright

Although we won't use Playwright in this chapter, it's a good idea to get it installed and verify that it's working.

Start by running npm test at the command line:

```
work/birthdays % npm test

> birthdays@0.0.1 test
> playwright test


Running 1 test using 1 worker

[WebServer]
[WebServer]
[WebServer] Generated an empty chunk: "hooks".
[WebServer]
  X  1 test.js:3:1 > index page has expected h1 (7ms)


  1) test.js:3:1 > index page has expected h1 ==========================
======================

    browserType.launch: Executable doesn't exist at /Users/daniel/
Library/Caches/ms-playwright/chromium-1041/chrome-mac/Chromium.app/
Contents/MacOS/Chromium


    ...
```

```
 1 failed
    test.js:3:1 > index page has expected h1 =========================
===================
```

If you've never installed Playwright before, you'll see a message like the preceding one.

Playwright has its own environment setup to do, such as installing Chromium onto your machine. You can install it with the following command:

```
npx playwright install
```

Then, trying npm test again should give you the following output, showing that the one example test that's included is passing:

```
> birthdays@0.0.1 test
> playwright test


Running 1 test using 1 worker

[WebServer]
[WebServer]
[WebServer] Generated an empty chunk: "hooks".
[WebServer]
  ✓  1 test.js:3:1 > index page has expected h1 (307ms)


  1 passed (4s)
```

This test, index page has expected h1, is a test for the "Welcome to SvelteKit" message you saw earlier when you launched the application in the browser.

Running Vitest

Running npm run test:unit is the default way to run Vitest tests. Try it now:

```
work/birthdays % npm run test:unit

> birthdays@0.0.1 test:unit
> vitest


 DEV  v0.25.8 /Users/daniel/work/birthdays

 ✓ src/index.test.js (1)
```

```
Test Files  1 passed (1)
     Tests  1 passed (1)
  Start at  15:56:18
  Duration  737ms (transform 321ms, setup 0ms, collect 16ms, tests
2ms)


 PASS  Waiting for file changes...
       press h to show help, press q to quit
```

This automatically puts you in watch mode, which means any changes to the filesystem will cause tests to re-run. Press *q* to quit this mode. I personally don't use watch mode and we won't be using it in this book. See the *Creating a shell alias* section for a little discussion on why this is.

In the next section, we'll make the ergonomics of the project a little easier for us.

Preparing your development environment for frequent unit testing

In this section, we'll take some configuration actions that will make our test-driven lives much simpler.

Choosing your editor

Let's start with your choice of code editor. More than likely, this means a choice between an IDE, such as Visual Studio Code, or a plain text editor, such as Vim or Emacs.

IDEs tend to have lots of bells and whistles and one of those is the built-in test runner, which runs tests for you and integrates test output into the editor itself. On the other hand, plain text editors will require you to have a separate Terminal window for you to enter test commands directly, as you did in the previous section.

Figure 1.1 shows how my own setup looks, using Vim and tmux to split windows. The top half of the screen is where I edit my source files, and when I'm ready to run tests, I can switch to the bottom half and enter the test command.

```
1 <script>                          1 import { describe, it, expect } from 'vitest';
2   export let name;                 2 import { render } from '@testing-library/svelte';
3 </script>                          3 import Hello from './Hello.svelte';
4                                     4
5 <p>Hello, {name}!</p>              5 describe('sum test', () => {
~                                     6   it('adds 1 + 2 to equal 3', () => {
~                                     7     expect(1 + 2).toBe(3);
~                                     8   });
~                                     9
~                                    10   it('renders hello into the document', () => {
~                                    11     document.body.innerHTML =
~                                    12       '<h1>Hello, world!</h1>';
~                                    13     expect(document.body).toHaveTextContent(
~                                    14       'Hello, world!'
~                                    15     );
~                                    16   });
~                                    17
~                                    18   it('renders hello, svelte', () => {
~                                    19     render(Hello, {
N..   src/Hello.svelte        5/5   src/index.test.js                       1/26
```

```
✓ src/index.test.js (3)
  ✓ sum test (3)
    ✓ adds 1 + 2 to equal 3
    ✓ renders hello into the document
    ✓ renders hello, svelte

 Test Files  1 passed (1)
      Tests  3 passed (3)
   Start at  12:33:18
   Duration  1.56s (transform 430ms, setup 147ms, collect 116ms, tests 13ms)

work/birthdays %
```

Figure 1.1 – Using tmux and Vim

Figure 1.2 shows the same project in Visual Studio Code with the Vitest extension installed. Notice the test runner has a bunch of neat features, such as the ability to filter the test output, and green ticks next to the line numbers of passing tests.

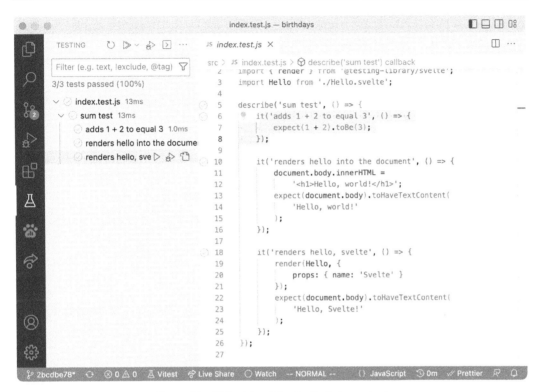

Figure 1.2 – Using Visual Studio Code to run tests

I think there is a lot to learn from using a plain editor and Terminal setup, but if you don't feel comfortable with that, then it's best to stick to your favorite IDE for now.

The one thing you want to make sure of is that it's easy and quick to run tests. So, if you're writing a new test, you want to immediately run it and see it fail. And if you're making a test pass or refactoring tests, make sure you can quickly re-run tests to check your progress.

Creating a shell alias

If you're choosing to use the Terminal to run tests, then you will almost certainly want to set up an alias to make it simpler to run Vitest unit tests. You'll recall that there are two commands that you use for running tests: `npm test` for Playwright tests and the `npm run test:unit` command for Vitest unit tests.

The style of testing shown in this book follows the classic *test pyramid* approach to testing, which states that we should have lots of little unit tests (in Vitest) and far fewer system tests (in Playwright).

So, given that we'll be working much more frequently with Vitest, doesn't it make sense to have the *shorter* `test` command be the one that runs unit tests?

The solution that I use is a shell alias, v, that invokes Vitest. If you wanted to use the standard watch mode, you'd set up the shell alias to run this command:

```
npx vitest
```

However, because I don't want to use watch mode, I set it up to use this command:

```
npx vitest run
```

I'd suggest you use this version, at least while you read through this book. I find that watch mode tends to break silently, especially when you're in the first stages of setting up a project. To avoid confusion, better to just invoke the test command when you're ready.

On my Mac, my default shell is zsh, which configures its shell aliases in the ~/.zshrc file. You can add that alias to the file using the following commands:

```
echo 'alias v="npx vitest run"' >> ~/.zshrc
source ~/.zshrc
```

Now, you can simply type the v command to run your Vitest unit tests. You can also use this to run a single test file, like this:

```
v src/index.tests.js
```

This is a handy way to run just a small part of your test suite.

Changing the test runner to report each test name

Recall that when we ran our Vitest unit tests, the test report told us the filename of the test suite that was run, together with some summary information:

```
DEV  v0.25.8 /Users/daniel/work/birthdays

✓ src/index.test.js (1)

Test Files  1 passed (1)
     Tests  1 passed (1)
  Start at  15:56:18
  Duration  737ms (transform 321ms, setup 0ms, collect 16ms, tests
2ms)
```

It turns out this isn't enough – we want to see test names too, just like how the Playwright test told us the description of the test that was passing.

Open the `vite.config.js` file and add a new `reporter` property that is set to `verbose`, as shown in the following code block:

```
const config = {
  plugins: [sveltekit()],
  test: {
    ...,
    reporter: 'verbose'
  }
};
```

> **Be careful**
>
> If you had left your test runner running in watch mode, you'll need to restart it at this point, and at any other point in which you modify the configuration.

Now, running tests at the command line using the v command will give this:

```
RUN   v0.25.8 /Users/daniel/work/birthdays

✓ src/index.test.js (1)
  ✓ sum test (1)
    ✓ adds 1 + 2 to equal 3

Test Files  1 passed (1)
     Tests  1 passed (1)
  Start at  11:02:05
  Duration  905ms (transform 320ms, setup 1ms, collect 16ms, tests
2ms)
```

Much better!

Watching the test fail

We're almost done with configuring Vitest, but before continuing, let's check that the test actually tests what we want it to test. This is an important concept with TDD: if you've never seen a test fail, how do you know it tests the right thing?

Open `src/index.test.js` and take a look:

```
import { describe, it, expect } from 'vitest';

describe('sum test', () => {
  it('adds 1 + 2 to equal 3', () => {
    expect(1 + 2).toBe(3);
```

```
    });
  });
```

Make a change to the expect statement, like the one shown here:

```
  expect(2 + 2).toBe(3);
```

Now if you run the test, you should see a failure:

```
❯ src/index.test.js:5:17
    3|  describe('sum test', () => {
    4|    it('adds 1 + 2 to equal 3', () => {
    5|      expect(2 + 2).toBe(3);
     |                         ^
    6|    });
    7|  });


  - Expected    "3"
  + Received    "4"
```

Brilliant – our test runner seems to be in working order. You can go ahead and undo the change to the test, and watch it go green again. That's it for the basic editor configuration.

Test file location – src or test?

In many other programming environments, test files are kept apart from application source files. A separate directory named something like tests or specs is used to house all executable test scripts.

There can be a couple of advantages to that. First, it can avoid packaging tests with application code when it comes to building deployable units. However, Svelte (and JavaScript in general) doesn't suffer from this problem because only modules referenced by the application entry point will be bundled.

Second, having a separate directory avoids the mindset of *one test file per module*. Not all modules need unit tests: if a unit exists as a part of a larger unit, we'll often just write tests for the top-level unit and those tests will also provide coverage for the lower-level unit. Conversely, sometimes it's helpful to have two (or more!) test files for a single module.

That's especially true when using component mocks that wipe out a component mock for an entire module. You might want a test file that mocks a component, and another test file where the component isn't mocked. We'll look at component mocks in *Chapter 12, Using Component Mocks to Clarify Tests*.

The current SvelteKit approach is to keep Vitest test files housed within the src directory. Partly, this is to avoid confusion with Playwright tests, which *do* live in a separate directory, named tests. (We'll see Playwright tests starting from *Chapter 3, Loading Data into a Route*).

This book continues with that style, but I would encourage you to explore and adopt whichever style you feel most comfortable with.

In the next section, we'll add support for the kinds of tests we'll be writing throughout the book.

Configuring support for Svelte component tests

A Svelte *component test* is one that, perhaps unsurprisingly, tests a Svelte component. For this, we need access to a **Document Object Model (DOM)**, which isn't part of the standard Node.js environment. We'll also need some additional packages for writing unit test expectations against the DOM.

Installing jsdom and testing library helpers

At the Terminal, run the following command to install the `jsdom` package and `@testing-library` packages that we'll use in our unit tests:

```
npm install --save-dev \
  jsdom \
  @testing-library/svelte \
  @testing-library/jest-dom \
  @testing-library/user-event
```

If you're using TypeScript, at this point, you may wish to add packages containing type definitions.

Next, create a new file named `src/vitest/registerMatchers.js` with the following content. It ensures that the matchers we'll be using are available for use via the `expect` function:

```
import matchers from '@testing-library/jest-dom/matchers';
import { expect } from 'vitest';

expect.extend(matchers);
```

Then, update `vite.config.js` to add a new `environment` property, which installs `jsdom` correctly, and also a `setupFiles` property, which ensures the file defined previously is loaded (and invoked) just before the test suites are loaded:

```
const config = {
  plugins: [sveltekit()],
  test: {
    ...,
    reporter: 'verbose',
    environment: 'jsdom',
    setupFiles: ['./src/vitest/registerMatchers.js']
  }
};
```

That's it for the basic setup. Now let's test it out.

Writing a test for the DOM

Open the `src/index.test.js` file and add the following test definition, inside the `describe` block. This test makes use of the `document` object that is created for us by the `jsdom` package, and the `toHaveTextContent` matcher that is provided by the `@testing-library/jest-dom` package:

```
it('renders hello into the document', () => {
  document.body.innerHTML =
    '<h1>Hello, world!</h1>';
  expect(document.body).toHaveTextContent(
    'Hello, world!'
  );
});
```

Now, if you run the test, you should see it pass. But, just as you did with the first test, it's important to confirm the test actually tests what it says it does. Change the test by commenting out or deleting the first line of the test, and then re-running the test runner.

You should see an output as follows:

```
 FAIL  src/index.test.js > sum test > renders hello into the document
Error: expect(element).toHaveTextContent()

Expected element to have text content:
  Hello, world!
Received:

❯ src/index.test.js:9:25
     7|
     8|  it('renders hello into the document', () => {
     9|    expect(document.body).toHaveTextContent(
      |                          ^
    10|      'Hello, world!'
    11|    );
```

That proves the test is working. You can go ahead and undo the breaking change you made.

Writing a first Svelte component test

Next, let's write an actual Svelte component and test that out. Create a new file named `src/Hello.svelte` with the following content:

```
<script>
  export let name;
</script>

<p>Hello, {name}!</p>
```

Then, go back to the `src/index.test.js` file and refactor your test to use this new component. To do that, replace the call to `document.outerHTML` with a call to the `render` function, like this:

```
it('renders hello into the document', () => {
  render(Hello, { name: 'world' });
  expect(document.body).toHaveTextContent(
    'Hello, world!'
  );
});
```

This `render` function comes from the `@testing-library/svelte` package. Import that now, along with an import for the `Hello` component, placed at the top of the file:

```
import { render } from '@testing-library/svelte';
import Hello from './Hello.svelte';
```

Check that the test still passes with the refactor.

Then, add this third test, which verifies that the `name` prop in the component is being used to verify the output:

```
it('renders hello, svelte', () => {
  render(Hello, { name: 'Svelte' });
  expect(document.body).toHaveTextContent(
    'Hello, Svelte!'
  );
});
```

Run the test and make sure it passes.

Now, go ahead and comment out the render call in the last test. You might think that the test fails with an error saying nothing was rendered on-screen. But let's see what happens:

```
Error: expect(element).toHaveTextContent()

Expected element to have text content:
  Hello, Svelte!
Received:
  Hello, world!
```

Hold on a second; is this what we expected? This test didn't ever print out a Hello, world! message so why is the test expectation picking it up?

It turns out that our tests share the same document object, which is clearly not good for test independence. Imagine if the second test also expected to see Hello, world! rather than Hello, Svelte!. It would have passed by virtue of the first test running. We need to do something about this.

Ensuring the DOM is cleared after each test run

We want to make sure that every test gets its own clean version of the DOM. We can do this by using the cleanup function.

Create a new file named src/vitest/cleanupDom.js:

```
import { afterEach } from 'vitest';
import { cleanup } from '@testing-library/svelte';

afterEach(cleanup);
```

Then, insert that into the setupFiles property in vite.config.js:

```
const config = {
  ...,
  test: {
    ...,
    setupFiles: [
      './src/vitest/cleanupDom.js',
      './src/vitest/registerMatchers.js'
    ]
  }
};
```

Now, if you run your failing test again, you should see that the Hello, world! message no longer appears.

Before continuing, uncomment the render call and check your tests are back in an all-green state.

Restoring mocks automatically

There's one final piece of configuration we need in `vite.config.js`. Add the `restoreMocks` property, as shown here:

```
const config = {
  ...,
  test: {
    ...,
    restoreMocks: true
  }
};
```

This is also important for test independence and will be important in *Chapter 11*, *Replacing Behavior with a Side-By-Side Implementation*, when we begin using the `vi.fn` function for building test doubles.

That covers all the configuration you need for the rest of the book. The next section touches briefly on some optional configurations you might want to consider.

Optional configuration

In this section, we'll look at configuring Prettier and setting up more appropriate tab widths on the Terminal. These settings mirror the print settings that are used in this book.

Configuring Prettier's print width

Due to the constraint of the physical pages in this book, I have set the `printWidth` setting of Prettier to 54 characters, and all code samples are formatted with that setting.

I also think the default value, `100`, is too high. I like short columns of text as I find them easier to share and read in all sorts of environments – such as on mobile devices, where it's much easier to scroll vertically than it is horizontally.

Also, having extra vertical space comes in handy when you are pairing with other developers and you want to refer to particular line numbers (assuming you have line numbers turned on).

In `.prettierrc`, you can set the print width with the following addition:

```
{
  "printWidth": 54,
  ...
}
```

You might be more comfortable with something in the `60` to `80` range.

Reducing the tab width in the Terminal

The Svelte community has a preference for tabs over spaces because tabs are better for screen readers. Unfortunately, a lot of Terminals and shell programs are set up for a default tab width of eight characters, which is way too many for my liking.

Although every Terminal is different, the one solid piece of advice I have is to set `git config` to use `less` as its pager, with tab stops at positions 1, 3, 5, and 7:

```
git config --global core.pager 'less -x1,3,5,7'
```

This makes `git diff` and `git show` much more bearable, and these are two commands I use extremely frequently.

Summary

This chapter has taken a detailed look at the various parts of a base SvelteKit project, showing how Playwright and Vitest are added, together with the additional dependencies you'll need to write Svelte component tests.

We've also looked at some of the ways you can set up your development environment to help you be productive.

You're now ready to start exploring TDD practices, starting with the *Red-Green-Refactor Cycle -> Workflow* in the next chapter.

2

Introducing the
Red-Green-Refactor Workflow

This chapter introduces the **Red-Green-Refactor** workflow, which is at the heart of **Test-Driven Development** (**TDD**). You'll use it to write a first Svelte component, including a unit-test suite that specifies the behavior of the component.

This workflow benefits you because it provides a structure for implementing software. It makes it less likely that you'll implement the wrong thing. It also helps you to avoid overcomplicating solutions.

This chapter covers the following topics:

- Understanding the Red-Green-Refactor workflow
- Thinking ahead with up-front design
- Writing a failing test
- Making it pass
- Refactoring the tests
- Adding styles to the component

By the end of the chapter, you'll have written your first pieces of Svelte functionality using TDD.

Technical requirements

The code for the chapter can be found online at `https://github.com/PacktPublishing/Svelte-with-Test-Driven-Development/tree/main/Chapter02/Start`.

Understanding the Red-Green-Refactor workflow

The Red-Green-Refactor workflow (or cycle) is a process that defines the mechanics of how you write software. It has enduring appeal because it has helped so many developers be more productive by providing structure to their day-to-day jobs.

You do your work by making repeated cycles through the workflow until your software is complete. Red-Green-Refactor also lends itself to pairs and groups of developers working together, because it gives you a way to organize your discussion and decision making.

Figure 2.1 shows the workflow. It has three parts:

- **Red**: To begin, you write a failing test. This sounds easier than it is, because first you have to know *what* you're intending to build.

- **Green**: Once you have a failing test, you make it pass. You strive to find the *shortest* route possible to solve the test.

- **Refactor**: Make it good. Take a step back and think about the design. Even though you took the shortest route there, did you make a mess? Are there any abstractions beginning to appear that can be made real, or are there existing abstractions that need to be adjusted?

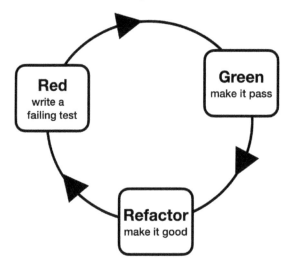

Figure 2.1 – The Red-Green-Refactor workflow

This gives you a structure for building software. You start from nothing, and by repeating the cycle, you build up your software product, test by test, until it does something useful. (Of course, you need to know your trajectory, but that is part of the first step, as we'll soon see.)

We'll look at the Red and Green steps in more detail in the two remaining parts of this chapter. First, we'll write some code to lend as an example, and then we'll discuss what we've done.

The third part, Refactor, is more easily explained when we have more code to play with, so we'll focus on that in *Chapter 4*, *Saving Form Data*, and *Chapter 5*, *Validating Form Data*.

You've now covered the theory behind Red-Green-Refactor. Let's try it out, shall we?

Thinking ahead with some up-front design

If you imagine that we are a team of developers embarking on a new project, it would be very unlikely that we'd start a project without a project brief – you can't just start writing tests with no purpose.

The goal of this section, therefore, is two things:

- Discuss, at a high level, what we'll build in the first part of the book
- Learn just enough so that we can write our first failing test

The Birthdays application

We will build a web application called *Birthdays* that manages a list of people and their birthdays.

Figure 2.2 shows this application in action. The main page is a list of birthdays that have been stored. At the bottom there's a form to add a new birthday, which is stored as a person's name (just a single text field) and their date of birth.

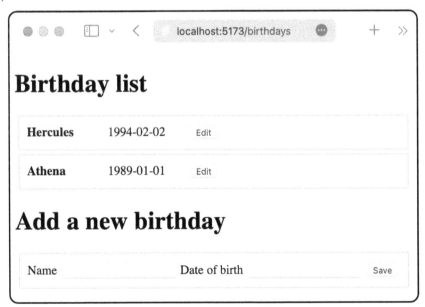

Figure 2.2 – The Birthdays application

The user accesses this application by navigating to the /birthdays URL of our website.

In this chapter, we'll focus on building a Svelte component that displays each birthday in a list. It can be used like this:

```
<Birthday name={name} dob={dob} />
```

We can start with a test that specifies what this `Birthday` component will do with its `name` prop.

Up-front design and TDD

The Red part of the workflow states *write a failing test*. Okay, but what test? In fact, every time you start the Red cycle, you should be thinking of your trajectory. What do we need next? What did we learn about our design? This is the *up-front design* that you should be doing before each test.

The trick, however, is doing *just enough* to know for certain what test you're writing. You don't need to have the whole system mapped out.

This is all the up-front design we need to do at this point. We know what we can make a start on – a check that the component displays the name.

Writing a failing test

In this section, you'll write your first unit test for the Vitest test runner.

Create a new file named `src/routes/birthdays/Birthday.test.js` and start with the following `import` statements:

```
import { describe, it, expect } from 'vitest';
import {
  render,
  screen
} from '@testing-library/svelte';
import Birthday from './Birthday.svelte';
```

The `describe` function is used to group tests into a suite of tests. Every test file (such as `Birthday.test.js`) will have at least one `describe` block. These blocks can also be nested; in future chapters, we'll look at a couple of scenarios where you'll want to do this. For example, in *Chapter 4, Saving Form Data*, you'll use them to group tests according to the individual form fields that appear within an HTML form.

The `it` function is a basic function for defining unit tests, and it is named this way so that the test description reads like a specification. The function is designed to be fluent, meaning its invocations should be read like plain English. That's generally something we aim for when writing tests, since it helps them to read like specifications.

The `expect` function is the one that we use to check our software did what we *expected* it to do.

The `render` and `screen` functions help us manipulate the **Document Object Model (DOM)** using our Svelte component: first, a call to `render` will output the component result into the current DOM document, and following that call, `screen` gives us a number of locator functions for finding DOM elements.

The final import is for the `Birthday` component. This component doesn't exist yet. In fact, the file doesn't exist yet. This is intentional. Notice how we've already made design choices: where the file should reside, what it's called, and what the component is named.

Design discussions at the unit level

If we were working together as a group, we'd have had a discussion about all these decisions. Although it might seem obvious, the TDD workflow gives us space to discuss these issues freely with our teammates.

Naming things is hard. That's why it really helps to discuss the naming. One thing I've learned about myself is that when I discuss a difficult variable name with others, we always come up with a better name than my own first choice.

Contrast this with being a solo developer, where you'd have your work reviewed after you'd completed it, perhaps packaged beautifully in a pull request. Imagine having done all the work only to be told later on by your teammates: *I think this name could be improved…* Frustrating, right? Having the discussion up front means you save yourself all that emotional turmoil later on.

Let's continue with writing the test. The first thing we need is the `describe` block and the `it` test description. Add the following just below the `import` definitions:

```
describe('Birthday', () => {
  it('displays the name of the person', () => {
  });
});
```

See how the descriptions given to the `describe` and `it` functions form a plain English sentence? *Birthday displays the name of the person.*

Now we can fill out the test:

```
describe('Birthday', () => {
  it('displays the name of the person', () => {
    render(Birthday, { name: 'Hercules' });
  });
});
```

The `render` call takes our `Birthday` component together with the `name` prop passed in. It will mount the `Birthday` component into the DOM, ready for us to check its result.

Next, it's time for the assertion. Complete the test with a call to the expect function, shown in the following code block:

```
describe('Birthday', () => {
  it('displays the name of the person', () => {
    render(Birthday, { name: 'Hercules' });

    expect(
      screen.queryByText('Hercules')
    ).toBeVisible();
  });
});
```

There are a couple of important things to note in this expectation.

First, note the use of the locator, screen.queryByText. The screen object has a whole bunch of query functions like this, all designed to find something individual elements in the DOM. We will uncover the common query functions as the book progresses. The queryByText function searches for the provided text and returns null if it isn't anywhere to be found.

---

queryBy versus getBy query function variants

If you have experience with Testing Library, you'll know that each of the query functions has a getBy and queryBy variant. When I'm using TDD, I use queryBy in the first test that introduces a new element. That makes it clear that I don't expect the element to exist yet. But once that test is green (and passing), subsequent tests can use getBy, which throws an exception if the element isn't found. This helps make it clear that this test depends on a previous test to prove the existence of the element.

The other important thing is the **matcher**: the toBeVisible function call that's chained off the expect function call. This checks that whatever we got in the first call is visible in the DOM document.

If you're familiar with Testing Library, you might be aware that there's a more functionally appropriate matcher that we could have used here. We could have used not.toBeNull, like this:

```
expect(
  screen.queryByText('Hercules')
).not.toBeNull();
```

I say this is more *functionally appropriate* because the queryByText query function will return null if it doesn't find the text on the page, and that's what we're really interested in here.

The reason I prefer toBeVisible is that it makes the test more readable, continuing with the theme of fluent, plain English matcher statements. Of course, it's also important to know what the failure messages look like when the test fails, which we're about to see.

The final step of the Red stage is watching the test fail. Go ahead and run it now, either in your IDE or on the Terminal. (If you followed the instructions for setting up in *Chapter 1, Setting up for Testing*, you will be able to run tests with either the v shell command or npm run test:unit.)

You should see output like the following:

```
FAIL  src/routes/birthdays/Birthday.test.js [ src/routes/birthdays/
Birthday.test.js ]
Error: Failed to load url ./Birthday.svelte (resolved id: ./Birthday.
svelte). Does the file exist?
```

This isn't actually a test failure! It's telling us the file we imported doesn't exist. This is the time to create it.

Go ahead and simply create a blank file at the src/routes/birthdays/Birthday.svelte location.

Then, rerun the tests. What happens?

```
FAIL  src/routes/birthdays/Birthday.test.js > Birthday > displays the
name of the person
Error: expect(received).toBeVisible()

received value must be an HTMLElement or an SVGElement.

> src/routes/birthdays/Birthday.test.js:13:5
    11|    expect(
    12|      screen.queryByText('Hercules')
    13|    ).toBeVisible();
      |           ^
    14|  });
    15| });
```

Perfect – we have a test failure! Note the cryptic message, received value must be an HTMLElement or an SVGElement. If we had instead used the not.toBeNull matcher, we would have seen something less cryptic. However, I think the test is simple enough that it's clear what's going on – especially because of this line:

```
Error: expect(received).toBeVisible()
```

This section has shown you how you can write a failing test using the basic describe, it, and expect functions. You've also seen how you can use the test runner to drive some of the plumbing work, such as creating files.

That completes the Red portion of the cycle. Next up: Green.

Making it pass

In this section, we'll make a very simple change to make the test pass, and then we'll repeat the cycle again with a second test.

To make this test pass, add the following content to the `src/routes/birthdays/Birthday.svelte` file:

```
<script>
  export let name;
</script>


<span><strong>{name}</strong></span>
```

Rerun your tests now, and you should see the following output from the Vitest test runner (you'll see the tests from *Chapter 1, Setting up for Testing*, are still listed here):

```
 √ src/routes/birthdays/Birthday.test.js (1)
   √ Birthday (1)
     √ displays the name of the person
 √ src/index.test.js (3)
   √ sum test (3)
     √ adds 1 + 2 to equal 3
     √ renders hello into the document
     √ renders hello, svelte

 Test Files  2 passed (2)
      Tests  4 passed (4)
   Start at  11:45:47
   Duration  1.60s (transform 503ms, setup 306ms, collect 272ms, tests
63ms)
```

Repeating the process

Let's go ahead and add a next step for the `dob` prop. Back in the `src/routes/birthdays/Birthday.test.js` file, add this test, just below the original test and still within the `describe` block:

```
it('displays the date of birth', () => {
  render(Birthday, { dob: '1994-02-02' });
  expect(
    screen.queryByText('1994-02-02')
  ).toBeVisible();
});
```

Make sure to run your test and watch it fail. Then, to make it pass, make the following additions to `src/routes/birthdays/Birthday.svelte`:

```
<script>
  export let name;
  export let dob;
</script>

<span><strong>{name}</strong></span>
<span>{dob}</span>
```

Run the tests again, and you should see both are now green. However, there are some warnings:

```
stderr | src/routes/birthdays/Birthday.test.js > Birthday > displays
the name of the person
<Birthday> was created without expected prop 'dob'

stderr | src/routes/birthdays/Birthday.test.js > Birthday > displays
the date of birth
<Birthday> was created without expected prop 'name'

 √ src/routes/birthdays/Birthday.test.js (2)
   √ Birthday (2)
     √ displays the name of the person
     √ displays the date of birth
```

We'll fix those warnings in the next section, along with addressing a couple of other issues.

Refactoring the tests

In this section, we'll look at some of the refactoring work we can do before we start thinking about the next feature. We'll start by fixing the test warnings from the last section, then we'll add a third test as a completeness test, and we'll finish by adding some styles.

Refactoring and changing behavior

The usual definition of refactoring is *any internal change that does not affect external behavior*. It is a bit of a stretch to include CSS style changes in this, or indeed changes that remove warnings. But I find that early on in a project, there are always little changes such as these ones that need to be made. The key point is that your test suite is *green* and remains *green* throughout.

Cleaning up warnings

It's important to clean up any warnings as they appear. That's because without doing this, the test runner output becomes full of noise. We want the output to be as short as possible so that it's quick to decipher any problems that occur.

In the `src/routes/birthdays/Birthday.test.js` file, add a new definition named `exampleBirthday` at the top of the `describe` block:

```
describe('Birthday', () => {
  const exampleBirthday = {
    name: 'Ares',
    dob: '1996-03-03'
  };
  ...
});
```

Then, update the first test to include this variable as the *base* props that are passed to the component:

```
it('displays the name of the person', () => {
  render(Birthday, {
    ...exampleBirthday,
    name: 'Hercules'
  });
  ...
});
```

Now update the second test, like this:

```
it('displays the date of birth', () => {
  render(Birthday, {
    ...exampleBirthday,
    dob: '1994-02-02'
  });
  ...
});
```

If you run your tests now, you should see the warnings have disappeared and the tests still pass.

Adding a third test to triangulate

What happens if you update the `Birthday.svelte` file to have hardcoded values like this?

```
<span><strong>Hercules</strong></span>
<span>1994-02-02</span>
```

Go ahead and try it; you'll find that your tests still pass.

In fact, your tests do not protect against hardcoding. This highlights an interesting facet of TDD. When we're building software guided by tests, we always aim to build the simplest thing that could possibly work.

To move beyond hardcoded values, we can add a second test for each individual property. Add this test to the test suite:

```
it('displays the name of another person', () => {
  render(Birthday, {
    ...exampleBirthday,
    name: 'Athena'
  });
  expect(
    screen.queryByText('Athena')
  ).toBeVisible();
});
```

You'll see that the hardcoded version no longer works. The simplest way to get both of these tests working is to simply output the name prop value passed in.

This section has covered a little bit of the Refactor step. There will be plenty more refactoring work as the book progresses.

Adding styles to the component

Finally, you can add the following `<style>` block to the `Birthday.svelte` file, which completes the `Birthday` component and means you'll be ready to display it on a page, which you'll do in the next chapter:

```
<script>
  export let name;
  export let dob;
</script>

<span><strong>{name}</strong></span>
<span>{dob}</span>

<style>
  span {
    display: inline-block;
    width: 100px;
  }
</style>
```

You can avoid writing unit tests for CSS since that is static information. Unit tests are specifically about behavior: what happens when this thing or that thing changes, or a different name prop is passed in?

Summary

This chapter has taken a detailed look at the steps involved in the Red-Green-Refactor workflow. You have seen how much thinking is involved in every single step, and how the TDD process provides a scaffold for both solo work and work as a team.

You have also seen how to create a Svelte component using TDD to write a unit test for the Vitest test runner.

The value of this kind of critical thinking is that it will help you map out your intended work from start to finish, removing the fear of going down a wrong path or getting lost. If you take time to practice this workflow, it will soon become second nature.

In the next chapter, we'll introduce Playwright testing, and you'll build a page to hold the Birthday component.

3
Loading Data into a Route

SvelteKit is very much about *routing*: figuring out what to display once your browser requests a page at a specific location. For example, the /birthdays route that we'll work on in this chapter. Part of that routing is ensuring that the route has the data available to it. In this chapter, you'll see how you can test-drive SvelteKit's load function for pulling that data into a component.

You'll also see how Playwright can be used to build an end-to-end test that proves all the various components of this system.

This chapter covers the following:

- Using Playwright to specify end-to-end behavior
- Deciding an approach to make the end-to-end test pass
- Test-driving the load function
- Test-driving the page component

By the end of the chapter, you'll have test-driven a functioning SvelteKit route that you can view in your web browser, and you'll have learned the key differences between Playwright end-to-end tests and Vitest unit tests.

Technical requirements

The code for the chapter can be found online at https://github.com/PacktPublishing/Svelte-with-Test-Driven-Development/tree/main/Chapter03/Start.

Using Playwright to specify end-to-end behavior

In this section, you will write your first Playwright test and learn about the various function calls within it, and you'll learn about differentiating between Playwright end-to-end tests and Vitest unit tests.

Writing the test and watching it fail

The test we are going to write is entitled `lists all birthdays` and it will perform the following steps:

1. Browse to the `/birthdays` location.

2. Look for the text `Hercules` and `Athena`, which it will take as evidence that the test has passed.

Once the test is in place, we'll stop to think about how this `Hercules` and `Athena` data should get into our system.

Create a new file named `tests/birthdays.test.js` and add the following content:

```
import { expect, test } from '@playwright/test';

test('lists all birthdays', async ({ page }) => {
  await page.goto('/birthdays');
  await expect(
    page.getByText('Hercules')
  ).toBeVisible();
  await expect(
    page.getByText('Athena')
  ).toBeVisible();
});
```

You can see some things here that are similar to the Vitest tests, such as the use of `expect` and the `toBeVisible` matcher.

However, some things are different. For a start, the test is marked as `async` and all the function calls (including the `expect` function calls) are marked with `await`.

That's necessary because Playwright is driving a headless browser, meaning it's started a real browser process that runs in the background and is invisible to you. Playwright has no mechanism for determining when the browser has completed working, beyond waiting patiently and frequently checking the browser state. Therefore, most of its internal logic is driven by waits and timeouts: the browser is given a certain amount of time, generally a few seconds, to get things displayed.

The `page.goto` call is instructing this headless browser to navigate to the `/birthdays` endpoint. Playwright takes care of spinning up a real dev server in the background and ensuring that any relative URLs (such as `/birthdays`) are converted to absolute URLs pointing at this dev server (like `https://localhost:5173/birthdays`).

Go ahead and run the test now, using the npm `test` shell command. You should see an almost immediate failure appear:

```
    1 birthdays.test.js:3:1 > lists all birthdays
  ✓ 2 test.js:3:1 > index page has expected h1 (618ms)
 [WebServer] Error: Not found: /birthdays
```

With the test complete, let's take a more detailed look at the difference between Vitest tests and Playwright tests.

Understanding the difference between Vitest tests and Playwright tests

There are fundamental differences between how Vitest tests work and how Playwright tests work. Both play their part in TDD.

Figure 3.1 shows how each type of test encompasses your code. Playwright tests are often referred to as end-to-end tests and they are high-level, with each test exercising a whole lot of code. Vitest tests are often called unit tests. They are very detailed and exercise just a small piece of the code.

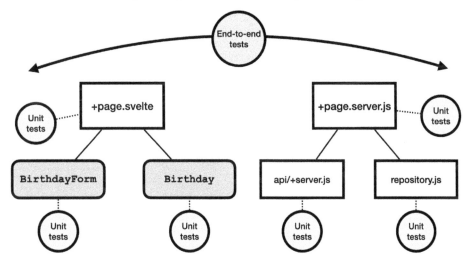

Figure 3.1 – End-to-end tests and unit tests in a SvelteKit project

Playwright tests are often a good starting point when embarking on building a new feature. They may even be written by project stakeholders who are not developers but still participate in defining features. In *Chapter 13, Adding Cucumber Tests*, we'll see how this can be done with plain English syntax rather than JavaScript code.

Playwright tests are often written against the browser UI. They exercise the whole system, including the web browser and any out-of-process resources such as databases. When working with a SvelteKit application, the Playwright test runner starts up the SvelteKit web server and executes all of the SvelteKit runtime code for managing routes.

In contrast, the Vitest test runner does not load up the SvelteKit web server and does not execute any of its code. Instead, it loads your JavaScript files directly into the same Node process that Vitest and your test suites are loaded into.

While Playwright tests are good for focusing a team on what needs to be built, they often have nothing to say about the internal design of the software or even the architecture of the system as a whole. This is where Vitest unit tests come in. They can be used by developers to work out the *how* of a system.

There are a number of ways that unit tests help with design. For example, if a unit test is proving difficult to write, that's sometimes a sign that the application design is too complex. Breaking apart the units in a different way can lead to the unit tests becoming much simpler.

Playwright tests are often kept low on specifics leaving the unit tests to cover the details. For example, in the test we just wrote, we are interested in the listing of the birthdays that the system knows about but notice that we only checked by looking for the names of people, and not the birthdays. We leave the complete birthday checks to the unit tests for the `Birthday` component, which we already wrote in *Chapter 2, Introducing the Red-Green-Refactor Workflow*.

This way, we end up with lots of low-level Vitest unit tests and a few higher-level Playwright tests. This is the classic test automation pyramid as described by Mike Cohn in the book *Succeeding with Agile*. It encourages a testing strategy that includes many unit tests, some service tests, and just a dollop of UI tests.

Figure 3.2 shows how the test automated pyramid can be applied to SvelteKit projects. Playwright end-to-end tests can be written against both the UI and also against specific API endpoints, and your unit tests are written for the Vitest runner.

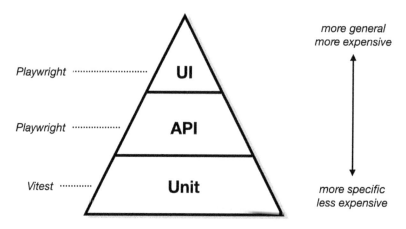

Figure 3.2 – The testing pyramid as applied to SvelteKit projects

One reason for structuring automated tests in this way is that unit tests are cheap to create and maintain, whereas UI tests are expensive in terms of time and energy put into them.

The service tests are like the UI tests in that they cover a whole flow through a system but avoid the UI. For example, they may call HTTP API endpoints directly. That can be helpful because the UI tends to be the most brittle component of the system, and driving a UI can take a while as you wait for the on-screen changes to be rendered.

> **Note**
>
> Modern web browser environments, together with modern test runners such as Playwright, have gotten much better at handling automated UI tests.

Another reason the classic test automation pyramid makes sense is that unit tests are often very fast to execute. You can have many unit tests, each of which executes just a tiny fraction of the code surface. When one of those tests breaks, it's very quick to read the test description or test code and figure out where in the application code the failure lies.

It's also worth remembering that unit tests serve to document all of the technical design decisions taken when writing the code, and this documentation is invaluable in understanding the history of a project.

Finally, keep in mind that Vitest unit tests do not test the SvelteKit server-side runtime environment. That means, for example, that a Vitest unit test can test that you correctly defined a `load` function, but it cannot test that the route is hooked up correctly. For that, you need a Playwright test that compiles and runs your components and routes just as if it was a real browser environment.

Deciding an approach to make the end-to-end test pass

With that all said, how do we begin writing Vitest unit tests now that we have a Playwright test that defines what we want?

The Playwright test looks for the names `Hercules` and `Athena`. The test makes an assumption that these two people have their birthdays listed in the system and that the page at `/birthdays` lists them. But how do we get them into the system in the first place?

In true TDD style, we can defer this decision and simply hardcode these two birthdays in the system. After all, the test doesn't seem to care about how the data gets into the system, only about how it is presented.

We can come back to how the birthdays are added later. In fact, we'll do this in *Chapter 8, Creating Matchers to Simplify Tests*. We can also make use of our `Birthday` component from *Chapter 2, Introducing the Red-Green-Refactor Workflow*, to display each birthday in turn.

Therefore, what we need to do is the following:

1. Create a `load` function that returns hardcoded birthday data for Hercules and Athena. This needs to exist within the `src/routes/birthdays/+page.server.js` file.

2. Create a `page` component that takes the data from `load` and displays a `Birthday` component for each of the birthdays given. This needs to exist as `src/routes/birthdays/+page.svelte`.

SvelteKit takes care of matching the `/birthdays` route to our files in the `src/routes/birthdays` directory. After calling `load`, it will pass the result into the `data` prop in the `+page.svelte` component.

That covers how to write a basic Playwright end-to-end test. We've discussed the differences between Playwright end-to-end and Vitest unit tests, and we've come up with a plan for the rest of the chapter.

The next section covers how to test-drive a basic, hardcoded version of our `load` function.

Test-driving the load function

Now that we've decided to implement a `load` function that returns hardcoded birthday data for Hercules and Athena, the actual change has become very simple.

The `load` function is a special SvelteKit function that will be invoked when a request comes in for the given route. So, when the user navigates to the `/birthdays` route, SvelteKit calls the `load` function in the `src/routes/birthdays/+page.server.js` file and then renders the component in the `src/routes/birthdays/+page.svelte` file.

Follow these steps to create the `load` function using TDD:

1. Create a new Vitest test file named `src/routes/birthdays/page.server.test.js` and start it off as shown. We are importing the `load` function from a `+page.server.js` file that doesn't yet exist. We call the function in our test and store the result:

    ```
    import { describe, it, expect } from 'vitest';
    import { load } from './+page.server.js';

    describe('/birthdays - load', () => {
      it('returns a fixture of two items', () => {
        const result = load();
      });
    });
    ```

Naming describe blocks for load functions

I've named the `describe` block `/birthdays - load`, which demonstrates a standard naming pattern that can be used for the `load` functions for routes.

---

2. Complete the test with the following expectation:

```
it('returns a fixture of two items', () => {
  const result = load();
  expect(result.birthdays).toEqual([
    { name: 'Hercules', dob: '1994-02-02' },
    { name: 'Athena', dob: '1989-01-01' }
  ]);
});
```

One expectation per test

This entire test contains just a single call to expect. Generally, when writing tests, I find it's useful to stick to just one expectation if possible. That helps to keep a strong link between the test description and the contents of the expect call.

It's often the case (as in this test) that you can stuff a whole lot of checks in a single expectation.

The toEqual matcher has a special *deep equality* mechanism that means each level of an object or array can be checked for its value, rather than its identity. And moreover, we can use constraint functions such as objectContaining, which we'll see in *Chapter 6, Editing Form Data*.

---

3. Go ahead and run the test with your Vitest test runner. This gives the following output:

```
FAIL  src/routes/birthdays/page.server.test.js [ src/routes/
birthdays/page.server.test.js ]
Error: Failed to load url ./+page.server.js (resolved id:
./+page.server.js). Does the file exist?
```

4. Do as it suggests and create an empty file at the src/routes/birthdays/+page.server.js location, and then rerun your tests. You should see the following:

```
FAIL  src/routes/birthdays/page.server.test.js > /birthdays -
load > returns a fixture of two items
TypeError: load is not a function
 > src/routes/birthdays/page.server.test.js:6:18
      4|  describe('/birthdays - load', () => {
      5|   it('returns a fixture of two items', () => {
      6|    const result = load();
       |                   ^
      7|    expect(result.birthdays).toEqual([
      8|     expect.objectContaining({
```

5. Okay, marvelous: load is not a function. Let's create a basic load function, then, with absolutely nothing in it. Add this to the new file:

```
export const load = () => ({});
```

6. Rerun your tests. You'll get the following:

```
FAIL  src/routes/birthdays/page.server.test.js > /birthdays -
load > returns a fixture of two items
AssertionError: expected [ { name: 'Hercules', …(2) }, …(1) ]
to deeply equal [ { name: 'Hercules', …(1) }, …(1) ]
 ❯ src/routes/birthdays/page.server.test.js:14:28
    12|   it('returns a fixture of two items', () => {
    13|     const result = load();
    14|     expect(result.birthdays).toEqual([
      |                              ^
    15|       { name: 'Hercules', dob: '1994-02-02' },
    16|       { name: 'Athena', dob: '1989-01-01' }

- Expected  - 10
+ Received  + 1

- Array [
-   Object {
-     "dob": "1994-02-02",
-     "name": "Hercules",
-   },
-   Object {
-     "dob": "1989-01-01",
-     "name": "Athena",
-   },
- ]"
+ "undefined"
```

7. To fix the issue, all we need to do is fill in the hardcoded values. Update the code in `src/routes/birthdays/+page.server.js` to look as follows:

```
export const load = () => ({
  birthdays: [
    { name: 'Hercules', dob: '1994-02-02' },
    { name: 'Athena', dob: '1989-01-01' }
  ]
});
```

Plumbing and hardcoded values

It may feel a bit pointless doing this, but the value is in getting the plumbing into place. The test we've written here will serve as a useful regression test when we come to fill in the *real* implementation, which does more than simply return hardcoded data. (We'll improve upon this implementation in *Chapter 4, Saving Form Data*).

---

8. Run your tests again and you'll see the test succeeds:

```
✓ src/routes/birthdays/page.server.test.js (1)
  ✓ /birthdays - load (1)
    ✓ returns a fixture of two items
```

That completes a working `load` function. You've now covered the basics of test-driving a route's `load` function so that it meets SvelteKit's requirements.

Now we can build the `page` component for the route.

Test-driving the page component

It's time to create the `page` component that exists for the route. As ever, we'll start with a test:

1. Create the `src/routes/birthdays/page.test.js` file and add the following imports. The last of these is for the `page` component itself. Because SvelteKit expects the component for a route to exist in a file named +page.svelte, we may as well give the component the name Page (that is what it is, after all):

```
import { describe, it, expect } from 'vitest';
import {
  render,
  screen
} from '@testing-library/svelte';
import Page from './+page.svelte';
```

2. Next, let's write out the test. The key part here is that Page gets passed a data prop, which needs to match the structure of our `load` function. In the actual runtime environment, SvelteKit will invoke the `load` function and then render the component in +page.svelte with the data prop set to the result of the `load` function:

```
describe('/birthdays', () => {
  const birthdays = [
    { name: 'Hercules', dob: '1994-02-02' },
    { name: 'Athena', dob: '1989-01-01' }
  ];

  it('displays all the birthdays passed to it', () =>
  {
    render(Page, { data: { birthdays } });
    expect(
      screen.queryByText('Hercules')
    ).toBeVisible();
    expect(
```

```
      screen.queryByText('Athena')
    ).toBeVisible();
  });
});
```

> **Test data fixtures**
>
> Even though they have the same values, there's no connection between the `birthdays` value set here and the hardcoded values in the `load` function. The `load` function will eventually lose its *seeded* data.

3. If you go ahead and run the test now, you should see the usual failure of the missing file:

    ```
    FAIL  src/routes/birthdays/page.test.js [ src/routes/birthdays/
    page.test.js ]
    Error: Failed to load url ./+page.svelte (resolved id: ./+page.
    svelte). Does the file exist?
    ```

4. Create an empty file at src/routes/birthdays/+page.svelte, and then run tests again:

    ```
    FAIL  src/routes/birthdays/page.test.js > /birthdays > displays
    all the birthdays passed to it
    Error: expect(received).toBeVisible()

    received value must be an HTMLElement or an SVGElement.
    ```

5. It's time for the real implementation. Copy the following code, which uses the `data` prop to display an `ol` element with a `li` for each birthday. We use the `Birthday` component from *Chapter 2, Introducing the Red-Green-Refactor Workflow*, to display the birthday for each item in the `data.birthdays` array:

    ```
    <script>
      import Birthday from './Birthday.svelte';

      export let data;
    </script>

    <h1>Birthday list</h1>
    <ol>
      {#each data.birthdays as birthday}
        <li>
          <Birthday {...birthday} />
        </li>
      {/each}
    </ol>
    ```

> **Using HTML lists for testability**
>
> When rendering *arrays* of items as we have here, it's always a good idea to use either an `ol` element (for an ordered list) or a `ul` element (for an unordered list) as the parent container, and then use `li` elements for each item in the list. Using list elements increases the testability of your components because you can use locator functions that look specifically for the `listitem` role, which we'll see in *Chapter 6, Editing Form Data*.

Notice also that we're using the `Birthday` component to make our tests pass. But our test didn't explicitly request a `Birthday` component; the expectations looked like this:

```
expect(
  screen.queryByText('Hercules')
).toBeVisible();
```

You could argue that the simplest way to make this test pass would be to simply print out the name of the birthday. But that would be ignoring the intent of our testing, which is to display a list of `Birthday` components.

In *Chapter 12, Using Component Mocks to Clarify Tests*, we will look at how we can use component mocks to explicitly state that we want to use a `Birthday` component here.

With the implementation complete, you can now verify your passing tests.

6. Run the Vitest test runner and you should see that the test is now passing:

```
✓ src/routes/birthdays/page.test.js (1)
  ✓ /birthdays (1)
    ✓ displays all the birthdays passed to it
```

7. You can now also run Playwright and see your passing test:

```
✓  1 test.js:3:1 > index page has expected h1 (402ms)
✓  2 birthdays.test.js:3:1 > lists all birthdays (430ms)


2 passed (4s)
```

8. You can add some styles to the `src/routes/birthdays/+page.svelte` file:

```
<style>
  ol {
    list-style-type: none;
    padding-left: 0;
  }

  li {
    padding: 10px;
```

```
        margin: 5px;
        border: 1px solid #ccc;
        border-radius: 2px;
      }
    </style>
```

9. Finally, run the dev server with npm run dev. Make a note of the base URL for your application and then fire up your browser, and load the /birthdays URL to check out your work.

> **Working out the path to load**
>
> The route we've built will end up at a location such as https://localhost:5173/birthdays. But the port number is likely to be different for you: you'll need to run the npm run dev command and look for the base URL that is marked with the Local label.

This section has shown you how you can test-drive a page component in a file named +page. svelte, which SvelteKit will render for you when you browse to a known route.

Summary

This chapter has shown you how to write an end-to-end test with Playwright and use that as a scaffold for your Vitest unit tests. The Playwright tests check that all the units are working together, and the framework is doing its job. The Vitest tests check that you are satisfying the contract required from SvelteKit, such as the load function working in the correct fashion.

You've also seen how TDD can be used to delay design decisions that aren't immediately relevant, like how we hardcoded sample data rather than implement any kind of persisted database of birthdays.

In the next chapter, we'll expand on the same ideas by implementing a SvelteKit form action, enabling you to add new birthdays to the list.

4

Saving Form Data

The preceding chapter introduced Playwright and SvelteKit routes. The data in our /birthdays route was hardcoded. In this chapter, we'll force the *real* implementation of the load function by adding the ability to add new birthdays into the system.

Figure 4.1 shows the new form we'll be building. It is attached to the bottom of the birthday list at the /birthdays route:

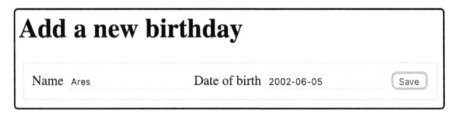

Figure 4.1 – The form for adding a new birthday

This chapter covers the following key topics:

- Adding a Playwright test for data input
- Test-driving a SvelteKit form
- Test-driving a SvelteKit form action

By the end of the chapter, you'll have a good understanding of how to test-drive SvelteKit forms.

Technical requirements

The code for the chapter can be found online at https://github.com/PacktPublishing/Svelte-with-Test-Driven-Development/tree/main/Chapter04/Start.

Adding a Playwright test for data input

Go ahead and add this test to `tests/birthdays.test.js`. It includes all the steps required for adding a new birthday to the system:

```
test('saves a new birthday', async ({ page }) => {
  await page.goto('/birthdays');
  await page.getByLabel('Name').fill('Persephone');
  await page
    .getByLabel('Date of birth')
    .fill('1985-01-01');
  await page.getByRole('button').click();
  await expect(
    page.getByText('Persephone')
  ).toBeVisible();
});
```

After navigating to the `/birthdays` endpoint, it uses the `getByLabel` locator function to find an `input` field that has a `Name` label. This is standard HTML functionality using the `label` and `input` elements, which we'll see in the next section.

We use the `fill` function to enter a value into this field, and then we repeat the process for the `Date of birth` field. Then, we click the button (any button!), and finally, we check that the `Persephone` text appears somewhere on the page.

An important distinction to make here is that `getByText` checks page text rather than, say, the values of the `input` fields. So, we can't just fill in the `Name` field and then watch the expectation magically pass.

The intent of the Playwright test is to show that the following steps are performed:

1. The user fills in a name and date of birth.
2. The user presses the **Save** button.
3. The system records the birthday in its system.
4. The browser refreshes the page, and the new birthday is displayed as part of the loaded page data.

With all that in mind, the process we'll use to make the test pass is as follows:

1. First, we'll build a new `BirthdayForm` component that displays a basic HTML form with two input fields and a button.
2. Then, we'll add this to the existing `+page.svelte` file that we built in the preceding chapter.
3. Finally, we'll add a form action to add this birthday, including introducing a new data structure to hold our birthdays in the server.

That covers our up-front design, all wrapped up in a Playwright test. Next, we can begin test-driving the form.

Test-driving a SvelteKit form

In this section, you'll construct a new component named `BirthdayForm`, together with its test suite. This component is an HTML form that comprises two text fields: `name` and `dob`. Each `input` element has a corresponding `label` element. There's also a button named **Save** that submits the form.

SvelteKit handles the submission of our form data from the client to the server. We won't test this behavior in our Vitest test suites, instead leaving it up to the Playwright tests to ensure that all pieces slot together correctly.

Follow these steps to build the new form:

1. Create a new file named `src/routes/birthdays/BirthdayForm.test.js` with the following first test. This uses the `queryByRole` query function to find an element with the `form` role on the page:

   ```
   import { describe, it, expect } from 'vitest';
   import {
     render,
     screen
   } from '@testing-library/svelte';
   import BirthdayForm from './BirthdayForm.svelte';

   describe('BirthdayForm', () => {
     it('displays a form', () => {
       render(BirthdayForm);
       expect(screen.queryByRole('form')).toBeVisible();
     });
   });
   ```

2. Make sure you run the test and watch it fail.

3. Then, create a new file named `src/routes/birthdays/BirthdayForm.svelte` with the following content:

   ```
   <form />
   ```

4. If you run tests now, you'll see the test still doesn't pass. That's because the `form` role only becomes available once you *name* a form. Update the implementation as follows:

   ```
   <form name="birthday" />
   ```

5. The test should now pass. Add the next test, as shown in the following code block. This test simply checks that we submit the form via a POST request, which is the usual mechanism for submitting new data to the server:

```
it('has a form method of POST', () => {
  render(BirthdayForm);
  expect(screen.getByRole('form').method).toEqual(
    'post'
  );
});
```

6. Make that pass by adding the method attribute, as shown here:

```
<form method="post" name="birthday" />
```

7. Then, add the third test, as shown in the following code block:

```
it('displays a button to save the form', () => {
  render(BirthdayForm);
  expect(
    screen.queryByRole('button')
  ).toBeVisible();
});
```

8. To make that pass, add an input element into the form with a type attribute set to submit. You can also give it value as Save, which will be used as the button name:

```
<form method="post" name="birthday">
  <input type="submit" value="Save" />
</form>
```

9. For the next test, we will introduce a nested describe block called name field. We can add a block here for grouping in anticipation of more tests for this field. We'll be adding some more in *Chapter 5*, *Validating Form Data*:

```
describe('name field', () => {
  it('displays a text field for the contact name', ()
  => {
    render(BirthdayForm);
    const field = screen.queryByLabelText('Name', {
      selector: 'input[type=text]'
    });
    expect(field).toBeVisible();
    expect(field.name).toEqual('name');
  });
});
```

This test makes use of the `queryByLabelText` function. This is analogous to the `page.getByLabel` function that was used in the Playwright test.

There is something else in this test that is important: the **cascading style sheets** (**CSS**) selector of `input[type=text]`. It's not very clear from the test, but the first expectation in this test checks all of the following:

- That a `label` element exists with the `Name` text
- That an `input` element exists with the `type` attribute set to `text`
- That the `label` element is associated with the `input` element

Part of these checks come from the selector expression itself. Without an explanation or understanding of the selector syntax, it's hard to know the intent behind this expectation.

There's also a second expectation in there to check that the name attribute is set. This is important so that the SvelteKit form action gets the right named parameters back. We'll add this parameter, `name`, and in the next test, we'll add another one named `dob`.

In *Chapter 8, Creating Matchers to Simplify Tests*, we'll refactor these expectations to improve their readability.

Let's carry on with the next steps:

1. To make the test pass, go ahead and add the `label` and `input` elements, as shown in the following code block:

   ```
   <form method="post" name="birthday">
     <label>
       Name
       <input type="text" name="name" />
     </label>

     <input type="submit" value="Save" />
   </form>
   ```

2. Now we can repeat the same thing with the `date of birth` field:

   ```
   describe('date of birth field', () => {
     it('displays a text field for the date of birth', ()
     => {
       render(BirthdayForm);
       const field = screen.queryByLabelText(
         'Date of birth',
         {
           selector: 'input[type=text]'
         }
   ```

```
    );
    expect(field).toBeVisible();
    expect(field.name).toEqual('dob');
  });
});
```

3. To make that pass, add in a field for the date of birth:

```
<form method="post" name="birthday">
  <label>
    Name
    <input type="text" name="name" />
  </label>

  <label>
    Date of birth
    <input type="text" name="dob" />
  </label>

  <input type="submit" value="Save" />
</form>
```

That completes the `BirthdayForm` component.

Adding the form component to the page component

Next, we'll add `BirthdayForm` into the existing page component for the `/birthdays` route:

1. Start by adding this test in `src/routes/birthdays/page.test.js`, as shown. We are testing for the presence of `BirthdayForm` simply by checking for an HTML element with the `form` role:

```
it('displays a form for adding new birthdays', () => {
  render(Page, { data: { birthdays } });
  expect(screen.getByRole('form')).toBeVisible();
});
```

Using previously prepared work to make tests pass

We *could* make this test pass by just adding a new `form` element, but given that we have `form` already prepared in `BirthdayForm`, it makes sense to use that. We'll see how component mocks can be used to make this test more specific in *Chapter 11, Replacing Behavior with a Side-By-Side Implementation.*

---

2. To make this pass, start by inserting the new `import` statement into `src/routes/birthdays/+page.svelte`:

```
<script>
    import Birthday from './Birthday.svelte';
    import BirthdayForm from './BirthdayForm.svelte';

    export let data;
</script>
```

3. Then, add a reference to the `BirthdayForm` component, together with a heading. Since the heading will remain static data, we don't need a test for that. Our Vitest tests are for *behavior* only – things that change when props change or **Document Object Model (DOM)** events fire:

```
<ol>
    ...
</ol>

<h1>Add a new birthday</h1>
<div>
  <BirthdayForm />
</div>
```

4. While you're here, you can also update the tag to make sure `div` has the same style as the `li` elements:

```
<style>
    ...

    li,
    div {
        ...
    }
</style>
```

You've now learned how to test-drive a form component and how to hook it up to your `page` component. That's it for the new `BirthdayForm` component, and if you load the dev server now and browse to the `/birthdays` URL, you should see the form displayed on the page.

In the next section, we'll wire up the **Save** button so that it adds the new birthday data into the system.

Test-driving a SvelteKit form action

The `form` action is the thing that SvelteKit calls when the form is submitted. It is defined in the `+page.server.js` file as an object named `actions`. The general form is shown in the following code block. Don't add this just yet; we'll come to it later on:

```
export const actions = {
  default: async ({ request }) => {
    const data = await request.formData();
    // ... do something with data here ...
  }
};
```

This is what we'll test-drive now. There's a few things to note:

- First, the Vitest unit tests can check the behavior of the `form` action, but it doesn't check any of the SvelteKit framework code that invokes the action. You'll recall we took the same approach with the HTML form: we didn't test the `submit` action since that magic is managed by SvelteKit. For testing the framework integration, we need the Playwright tests.

- Second, if you take a look at the preceding code sample, the form action has an action parameter with a `formData` function. This returns an item of the `FormData` type, which is a built-in DOM type.

- If we're going to test the `form` action, we'll need a way to build these `FormData` objects.

What we'll do is create factory methods to generate example objects for use in our tests. After that, we'll build our form action. However, in order to do that, we'll need to replace our hardcoded load function with a *real* implementation.

Building a factory for the FormData objects

Create a new file named `src/factories/formDataRequest.js` and add the following function:

```
const createFormDataFromObject = (obj) => {
  const formData = new FormData();
  Object.keys(obj).forEach((k) =>
    formData.append(k, obj[k])
  );
  return formData;
};
```

This function takes a plain JavaScript object and converts it into a `FormData` object by repeatedly calling the append method with each of the `obj` key-value pairs

Next, add the `createFormDataRequest` function, as shown in the following code block. It returns a SvelteKit request object that behaves in the same way that SvelteKit will:

```
export const createFormDataRequest = (obj) => ({
  formData: () =>
    new Promise((resolve) =>
      resolve(createFormDataFromObject(obj))
    )
});
```

You can now use this within your Vitest tests for the form action.

Building a Vitest test suite for the form action

Open the `src/routes/birthdays/page.server.test.js` file and update `load` import to also import the `actions` object:

```
import { load, actions } from './+page.server.js';
```

Just below that, add a new `import` statement for the `createFormDataRequest` factory that you just defined:

```
import {
  createFormDataRequest
} from 'src/factories/formDataRequest.js';
```

Then, at the bottom of the file, in a new top-level describe block, add the following test:

```
describe('/birthdays - default action', () => {
  it('adds a new birthday into the list', async () => {
    const request = createFormDataRequest({
      name: 'Zeus',
      dob: '2009-02-02'
    });

    await actions.default({ request });

    expect(load().birthdays).toContainEqual(
      expect.objectContaining({
        name: 'Zeus',
        dob: '2009-02-02'
      })
    );
  });
});
```

This test builds a request, calls our form action with it, and then uses the `load` function to check that it's returned successfully. But there's a difficulty here. Because our `load` function from the preceding chapter had a hardcoded implementation, there's no way for us to add any new data there.

Before we can make this test pass, we need to replace our hardcoded `load` function with a version that will then make this test easy to pass.

Skipping tests as part of a TDD workflow

Sometimes, we write a *Red* test and are ready to make it *Green*. But the approach to making it *Green* involves a whole bunch of refactoring. In these scenarios, it is better to rewind by marking the new *Red* test as skipped. Then you can safely refactor while you are on *Green*. Once your refactor is complete, un-skip your test, and you're back on *Red*. Now make the test pass given all your refactoring work is done.

Why go through this dance? Because you have the safety of a fully *Green* test suite to tell whether your Refactor has been completed correctly or not.

Start by skipping the test you just added, like this:

```
it.skip('adds a new birthday into the list', async () => {
  ...
});
```

Re-run all your tests to check that they are passing, except for the skipped test:

```
✓ src/routes/birthdays/page.server.test.js (2)
  ✓ /birthdays - load (1)
    ✓ returns a fixture of two items
  ↓ /birthdays - default action (1) [skipped]
    ↓ adds a new birthday into the list [skipped]
...
Test Files  5 passed (5)
     Tests  15 passed | 1 skipped (16)
```

Now in the `src/routes/birthdays/+page.server.js` file, update the implementation to read as follows:

```
const db = [];

const addNew = (item) => db.push(item);

addNew({ name: 'Hercules', dob: '1994-02-02' });
addNew({ name: 'Athena', dob: '1989-01-01' });
```

```
export const load = () => ({
    birthdays: Array.from(db)
});
```

This new implementation gives us an addNew function that we can use in our latest test.

Re-run all tests and check that they have passed. Then, you can un-skip the latest test and re-run it. You should get a failure, as shown in the following block:

```
FAIL  src/routes/birthdays/page.server.test.js > /birthdays - default
action > adds a new birthday into the list
TypeError: Cannot read properties of undefined (reading 'default')
 > src/routes/birthdays/page.server.test.js:22:17
    20|   });
    21|
    22|   await actions.default({ request });
```

Okay; we can just add an empty default function to get started. Add the following to the bottom of the src/routes/birthdays/+page.server.js file:

```
export const actions = {
  default: async ({ request }) => {
  }
};
```

If you run the tests again, you'll see from the failure that all the plumbing seems fine; it's just that we're missing the important call to add the birthday:

```
FAIL  src/routes/birthdays/page.server.test.js > /birthdays - default
action > adds a new birthday into the list
AssertionError: expected [ { name: 'Hercules', …(1) }, …(1) ] to deep
equally contain ObjectContaining{ …(3) }
 > src/routes/birthdays/page.server.test.js:24:28
    22|   await actions.default({ request });
    23|
    24|   expect(load().birthdays).toContainEqual(
      |                            ^
    25|     expect.objectContaining({
    26|       name: 'Zeus',

  - Expected   - 4
  + Received   + 10

  - ObjectContaining {
  -   "dob": "2009-02-02",
  -   "name": "Zeus",
```

```
  - }"
...
```

Finally, make the test pass by adding the call to the addNew function that already exists:

```
export const actions = {
  default: async ({ request }) => {
    const data = await request.formData();
    addNew({
      name: data.get('name'),
      dob: data.get('dob')
    });
  }
};
```

Re-run your tests; the tests should all be passing now. And if you run the Playwright test, you should find it also passes:

```
[WebServer]
  ✓  1 test.js:3:1 > index page has expected h1 (499ms)
  ✓  2 birthdays.test.js:3:1 > lists all birthday (507ms)
  ✓  3 birthdays.test.js:13:1 > saves a new birthday (309ms)


  3 passed (5s)
```

Now would be a great time to fire up the dev server and try the form out for real.

You've now learned how to test-drive a SvelteKit form action, completing the last stage of work needed to fully test-drive an entire route.

Summary

This chapter has covered how to test-drive SvelteKit forms and form actions using both Playwright end-to-end tests and Vitest unit tests.

You have seen how Vitest is useful for testing all the peculiarities of individual Svelte components but isn't good at testing the framework code of SvelteKit, such as the code that takes an HTML form submit event, builds a server request, and invokes your form action. For that, you need a Playwright test.

In the next chapter, you'll build on this form by adding some server-side form validations.

5

Validating Form Data

Now that our system is accepting new birthdays, we need to validate the data coming in. In this chapter, we'll see how we can test-drive the SvelteKit `fail` function to return useful information to the user so that they can correct any errors.

Figure 5.1 shows what is displayed to the user after the server has deemed their date of birth invalid. Notice how the invalid form data is maintained so that the user has a chance to correct it:

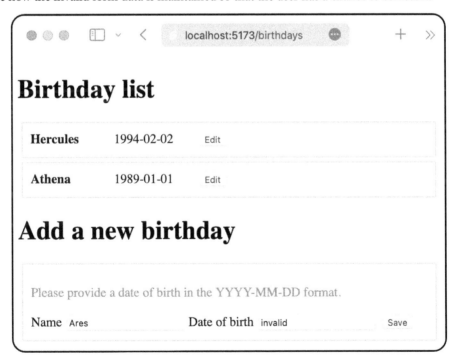

Figure 5.1 – A validation error is shown when entering an invalid date

This chapter covers the following key topics:

- Adding a Playwright test for validating form errors
- Displaying SvelteKit form errors
- Validating data in the form action
- Clearing the data store between tests

By the end of the chapter, you'll have a good understanding of how to implement form validation using a test-driven approach.

Technical requirements

The code for the chapter can be found online at `https://github.com/PacktPublishing/Svelte-with-Test-Driven-Development/tree/main/Chapter05/Start`.

Adding a Playwright test for validating form errors

In this section we'll write another Playwright test and then do some up-front planning for the Vitest unit tests we'll need.

Here's the next end-to-end test, which you can now add to `tests/birthdays.test.js`. It fills in the birthday form, just as in the previous chapter, but this time, the **Date of birth** field value is `invalid`: it is, literally, the word `invalid`, which is not a valid date of birth:

```
test('does not save a birthday if there are validation errors', async
({
  page
}) => {
  await page.goto('/birthdays');
  await page.getByLabel('Name').fill('Demeter');
  await page
    .getByLabel('Date of birth')
    .fill('invalid');
  await page.getByRole('button').click();
  await expect(
    page.getByText('Demeter')
  ).not.toBeVisible();
  await expect(
    page.getByText(
      'Please provide a date of birth in the YYYY-MM-DD
      format.'
    )
```

```
  ).toBeVisible();
});
```

Let's think about the error message for a second: `Please provide a date of birth in the YYYY-MM-DD format`. In the interest of brevity, we're not going fully test-drive this; rather, we'll just accept anything that can be parsed by the in-built `Date.parse` function. It turns out that a lot of strings can be parsed by this function.

Beyond that, what else will be needed to make this work? Our form action should use SvelteKit's `fail` function to signal to SvelteKit that the form needs to be re-evaluated. We call it with an **HTTP response code**, such as `422` – the *Unprocessable entity* error code – meaning the request data was invalid.

The `fail` function can also return an object that is passed back to the client. It is given to our page component as a `form` prop. The object is a plain JavaScript object that we control. We can return whatever we want in it: all we have to do is call SvelteKit's `fail` function with the object, and it will return that to the client.

Valid return objects

The return object is only valid if it can be serialized into a string and reconstructed in the browser. Functions can't be serialized, so they can't be passed back.

We can include an `error` property that returns an error message. We can also return the `name` and `dob` properties so that they can be presented to the user again.

An example object looks like this:

```
{
  name: 'Demeter',
  dob: 'invalid',
  error: 'Please provide a date of birth in the YYYY-MM-DD
          format.'
}
```

In the remaining sections, we'll start by updating the `BirthdayForm` component to make use of this new `form` prop. Then, we'll update the form action to return the validation errors for two different validation errors: an empty name and an invalid date of birth.

Displaying SvelteKit form errors

In this section, we'll add tests and functionality to support passing in a new `form` prop into the `BirthayForm` component.

Let's start with a new test:

1. In the `src/routes/birthdays/BirthdayForm.test.js` file, add a new nested `describe` block with a single test, as shown in the following code snippet. It checks that if the `error` property is set on the `form` prop, then that error must be displayed somewhere on the page:

```
describe('validation errors', () => {
  it('displays a message', () => {
    render(BirthdayForm, {
      form: {
        error: 'An error'
      }
    });
    expect(
      screen.queryByText('An error')
    ).toBeVisible();
  });
});
```

2. Make that pass in `src/routes/birthdays/BirthdayForm.svelte`, first by adding an `export` statement for the new `form` prop and then by adding a new p element with the error text. You can also add the `<style>` element at the bottom, although this isn't necessary for the test to pass:

```
<script>
  export let form;
</script>

<p class="error">{form.error}</p>

<form>
  ...
</form>

<style>
  .error {
    color: red;
  }
</style>
```

3. If you run tests now, you'll see we've broken a bunch of other tests by requiring the `form` prop to have an object value. But for the *create* mode of this component, the `form` prop should remain undefined. Update the `BirthdayForm` component as shown in the following code block:

```
<script>
  export let form = undefined;
</script>

{#if form?.error}
  <p class="error">{form.error}</p>
{/if}

...
```

4. Let's add the next test in the same `describe` block. This test checks that if an error occurs, we re-populate the `name` text field with the same value as was passed in:

```
describe('validation errors', () => {
  ...
  it('keeps the previous name value when an error
  occurs', () => {
    render(BirthdayForm, {
      form: {
        name: 'Hercules',
        error: 'Some awful error message'
      }
    });
    expect(
      screen.queryByLabelText('Name')
    ).toHaveValue('Hercules');
  });
});
```

5. To make that pass, simply add a `value` attribute value to the `input` field:

```
<input type="text" name="name" value={form?.name} />
```

6. Now repeat that for the `dob` field:

```
describe('validation errors', () => {
  ...
  it('keeps the previous dob value when an error
  occurs', () => {
    render(BirthdayForm, {
      form: {
```

```
          dob: '1994-01-01',
          error: 'Some awful error message'
        }
      });
      expect(
        screen.queryByLabelText('Date of birth')
      ).toHaveValue('1994-01-01');
    });
  });
```

7. Make that pass by adding the `value` attribute on the dob field:

```
<input type="text" name="dob" value={form?.dob} />
```

8. If you run the app now, you'll see that in *create* mode, the `undefined` string value now appears for the **Name** and **Date of birth** fields. That's because `form` is `undefined` in *create* mode, and therefore `value` is `undefined`. And the browser converts that to a string, giving `undefined` in the text box. To fix that, we need to specify an initial value for the fields. In the `BirthdayForm` test suite, find the `describe` block for the name field and add a second test into it, as shown in the following code block:

```
describe('name field', () => {
  ...
  it('initially has a blank value', () => {
    render(BirthdayForm);
    expect(
      screen.getByLabelText('Name')
    ).toHaveValue('');
  });
});
```

9. To make that pass, update the `value` attribute, like this:

```
<input
  type="text"
  name="name"
  value={form?.name || ''}
/>
```

10. Then, repeat that for `date of birth field`, starting with the test shown here:

```
describe('date a birth field', () => {
  ...
  it('initially has a blank value', () => {
    render(BirthdayForm);
    expect(
      screen.getByLabelText('Name')
```

```
    ).toHaveValue('');
  });
});
```

11. Finally, make that test pass by setting the `value` attribute on the `dob` field in the same way:

```
<input
  type="text"
  name="dob"
  value={form?.dob || ''}
/>
```

That completes the `BirthdayForm` component changes. Next, we need to get the `form` prop into `BirthdayForm` from the page component.

Passing the form data through the page component

The `BirthdayForm` component is not the *root* route component: it is instantiated as a child component from the component in +page.svelte.

Follow these steps to ensure that the `form` prop is received by the `page` component and passed into the `BirthdayForm` component:

1. In `src/routes/birthdays/page.test.js`, add a new test at the bottom of the test suite, as shown in the following code snippet. It checks that if the `form` prop is sent with the `error` prop, the `error` text appears onscreen:

```
it('passes any form information to the BirthdayForm', () => {
  render(Page, {
    data: { birthdays },
    form: { error: 'An error' }
  });
  expect(
    screen.queryByText('An error')
  ).toBeVisible();
});
```

2. Because the page component is already rendering `BirthdayForm`, it turns out the simplest way to make this test pass is to pass the `form` prop into `BirthdayForm`. In *Chapter 12, Using Component Mocks to Clarify Tests*, we'll see how this test can be rewritten using component mocks. For now, though, in `src/routes/birthdays/+page.svelte`, update the component to declare the `form` prop, and then pass it directly into `BirthdayForm`:

```
<script>
  ...
  export let form = undefined;
```

```
</script>

...

<BirthdayForm {form} />
```

You've now learned how to use automated tests to drive the display of form errors.

In the next section, we'll write tests for the form action that occurs on the server side.

Validating data in the form action

Now we're all set up for errors on the client, but we need the server code to actually do the validation checks. We'll add two checks: one to check that the name is not empty, and one to check that the date can be parsed into a valid `Date` object.

Each of these checks needs four unit tests: the first to ensure we break early without adding the birthday; the next to check the `422` error code; then one to check the error message text; and finally, one to check that the original data is passed back. (In *Chapter 8, Creating Matchers to Simplify Tests*, you'll see how to build a matcher that will roll up three of these tests into one single test.)

The beforeEach function

This section introduces the `beforeEach` function, which is used to run setup code before each of the tests within the `describe` block. It is a useful tool for reducing duplication within your test suites. You can consider it as part of the **Arrange** phase of your tests.

The `beforeAll`, `afterEach`, and `afterAll` functions do similar jobs but are used less frequently. We used the `afterEach` function for initialization in *Chapter 1, Setting up for Testing*, and we'll use `beforeAll` in *Chapter 8, Creating Matchers to Simplify Tests*.

Let's get started:

1. In `src/routes/birthdays/page.server.test.js`, add a new import for the `beforeEach` function. We'll use this to perform the setup for an entire set of tests:

    ```
    import {
      describe,
      it,
      expect,
      beforeEach
    } from 'vitest';
    ```

Then add a nested `'validation errors'` describe block, together with another nested describe block entitled `'when the name is not provided'`, as shown here. This includes the first test, too:

```
describe('/birthdays - default action', () => {
  ...
  describe('validation errors', () => {
    describe('when the name is not provided', () => {
      let result;

      beforeEach(async () => {
        const request = createFormDataRequest({
          name: '',
          dob: '2009-02-02'
        });

        result = await actions.default({
          request
        });
      });

      it('does not save the birthday', () => {
        expect(load().birthdays).not.toContainEqual(
          expect.objectContaining({
            name: '',
            dob: '2009-02-02'
          })
        );
      });
    });
  });
});
```

The when… context

The `when` style of naming the `describe` contexts is common when a group of tests belongs to a specific starting scenario, such as the one shown in the preceding scenario. They often have a `beforeEach` block that contains a setup that is common to all the tests.

It can sometimes be tempting to have multiple levels of nesting, but for simplicity, it's best to keep a single level of the `when...` context blocks. The preceding example shows an outer block named `'validation errors'`, but that is for organization only and contains none of its own setup.

2. Then, in the `src/routes/birthdays/+page.server.js` file, update `actions` with
    a new **guard clause** that returns from the function early if the `name` field is empty:

    ```
    export const actions = {
      default: async ({ request }) => {
        const data = await request.formData();
        const name = data.get('name');

        if (empty(name)) {
          return;
        }

        ...

      }
    };
    ```

3. For that to work, you'll need a definition of the `empty` function, which you can define as shown:

    ```
    const empty = (value) =>
      value === undefined ||
      value === null ||
      value.trim() === '';
    ```

> **Taking shortcuts**
>
> You might observe that we haven't fully tested the `empty` function, such as what happens if a
> line of spaces is sent in. To avoid having to write even more tests within this chapter, I've not
> written out those tests. If this were a real application, I'd move `empty` to a file of its own and
> then provide a whole bunch of unit tests that run directly against it.

4. For the next test, we'll write a test that ensures the form returns a `422` response. Add this test
    into the same nested `describe` block:

    ```
    it('returns a 422', () => {
      expect(result.status).toEqual(422);
    });
    ```

5. To make that pass, first add the following `import` statement in the `src/routes/`
    `birthdays/+page.server.js` file:

    ```
    import { fail } from '@sveltejs/kit';
    ```

6. Then update the guard clause to return a value using `fail`:

```
if (empty(name)) {
  return fail(422);
}
```

7. Now, still in the same nested `describe` block, add a test for the error message:

```
it('returns a useful message', () => {
  expect(result.data.error).toEqual(
    'Please provide a name.'
  );
});
```

8. Make that pass by adding a `return` object as the second parameter to the `fail` call:

```
if (empty(name)) {
  return fail(422, {
   error: 'Please provide a name.'
  });
}
```

9. Then add the final test for this name check, which is that we continue to pass the `dob` field value back, too:

```
it('returns the data back', () => {
  expect(result.data).toContain({
    dob: '2009-02-02'
  });
});
```

10. Complete the guard clause, as shown in the following code snippet. For this, you'll need to pull out the `dob` field in the same way you did with `name`:

```
const name = data.get('name');
const dob = data.get('dob');

...

if (empty(name)) {
  return fail(422, {
    dob,
    error: 'Please provide a name.'
  });
}
```

11. Now let's start on the second check for a `date` value that can't be parsed. This behaves exactly the same as the previous check, just with different values for the form data:

```
describe('/birthdays - default action', () => {
  ...
  describe('validation errors', () => {
    ...
    describe('when the date of birth is in the wrong
    format', () => {
      let result;

      beforeEach(async () => {
        const request = createFormDataRequest({
          name: 'Hercules',
          dob: 'unknown'
        });

        result = await actions.default({
          request
        });
      });

      it('does not save the birthday', () => {
        expect(load().birthdays).not.toContainEqual(
          expect.objectContaining({
            name: '',
            dob: '2009-02-02'
          })
        );
      });
    });
  });
});
```

12. To make that pass, first define an `invalidDob` helper next to the `empty` helper:

```
const invalidDob = (dob) => isNaN(Date.parse(dob));
```

13. Then, update the form action with a new guard clause:

```
export const actions = {
  default: async ({ request }) => {
    ...
```

```
        if (invalidDob(dob)) {
            return;
        }
    }
};
```

14. Then, repeating the motions from *step 4* onwards, add a test to ensure that a 422 response is returned:

```
it('returns a 422', () => {
    expect(result.status).toEqual(422);
});
```

15. To make that pass, update the `return` statement like this:

```
if (invalidDob(dob)) {
    return fail(422);
}
```

16. Next, add a test for a useful message to be returned:

```
it('returns a useful message', () => {
    expect(result.data.error).toEqual(
        'Please provide a date of birth in the YYYY-MM-DD
        format.'
    );
});
```

17. Update the guard clause to display that message:

```
if (invalidDob(dob)) {
    return fail(422, {
        error:
            'Please provide a date of birth in the YYYY-MM-
            DD format.'
    });
}
```

18. For the final test, we check that *all* the data is returned, including the invalid date. This is so that the user has the opportunity to correct the data:

```
it('returns all data back, including the incorrect value', () =>
{
    expect(result.data).toContain({
        name: 'Hercules',
        dob: 'unknown'
```

```
      });
    });
```

19. And make that pass by passing in the `name` and `dob` properties to the failure object. At this point, all your tests should be passing:

```
if (invalidDob(dob)) {
  return fail(422, {
    name,
    dob,
    error:
        'Please provide a date of birth in the YYYY-
        MM-DD format.'
  });
}
```

20. Now, as a final, tiny *refactor* step, you can update the call to `addNew` so that it uses the form data values that you've already pulled out from previous steps:

```
addNew({
  name,
  dob
});
```

That completes test-driving the server-side validation. Your Vitest tests and the Playwright test will now pass. You can also try out the app by running the dev server (with the `npm run dev` command) and opening your browser.

In the final section of this chapter, we'll fix a bug that's crept into our test suites.

Clearing the data store between tests

It turns out our tests are not independent: changes to the `db` object in one test affect the other tests, too. We have to clear down our test database between each run. We can solve that by creating a `clear` function that will clear the database object, and we'll use a `beforeEach` block to call it before every test.

What we need is the `clear` function that we can call directly in our tests. However, if you try to add this function to the `+page.server.js` file, you'll get a warning from SvelteKit when you run your Playwright tests:

```
Error: Invalid export 'clear' in /birthdays (valid exports are load,
prerender, csr, ssr, actions, trailingSlash, or anything with a '_'
prefix)
```

Why does this error appear only in the Playwright tests and not the Vitest tests? Your Vitest tests do not run through the SvelteKit server code, so the framework has no opportunity to check for invalid exports. It's only when you run tests via Playwright that you'll see runtime issues such as this.

SvelteKit only wants a `load` export and an `actions` export and absolutely nothing else. So, we need to move things out of the action and into their own file:

1. Create a new file, `src/lib/server/birthdayRepository.js`, with the following content:

    ```
    let db = [];

    export const addNew = (item) => db.push(item);

    export const getAll = () => Array.from(db);

    export const clear = () => (db = []);
    ```

2. In `src/routes/birthdays/+page.server.js`, you can now import those, as shown in the following code block. Note the use of the $ symbol in front of the file path, which is used to make a location that is relative to the `src` folder, which avoids us having to write `../../` before the filename:

    ```
    import {
      addNew,
      getAll
    } from '$lib/server/birthdayRepository.js';
    ```

3. Then delete the `db` and `addNew` functions and update the `load` function to read as follows. At this point, all your tests (except for the skipped one) should still be passing:

    ```
    export const load = () => ({
      birthdays: getAll()
    });
    ```

4. Now you can add this new `import` statement in `src/routes/birthdays/page.server.test.js`:

    ```
    import
      as birthdayRepository
    from '$lib/server/birthdayRepository.js';
    ```

5. Add in the `beforeEach` statement, as shown in the following code block:

    ```
    describe('/birthdays - default action', () => {
      beforeEach(birthdayRepository.clear);

      ...
    });
    ```

6. Finally, in the action `describe` block, you can now also replace the use of `load` with `birthdayRepository.getAll`, which makes the test a little clearer as to what's actually being tested: that the form action causes a new birthday to be inserted into the `birthdayRepository` object:

    ```
    it('adds a new birthday into the list', async () => {
      . . .
      expect(birthdayRepository.getAll()).toContainEqual(
        . . .
      );
    });
    ```

In the last step, take care not to replace *all* the occurrences of `load`. In the second `describe` block, it's the `load` function that is the function under test. Therefore, we keep those tests exactly as they are.

That completes all the work involved in extracting the repository module. Doing so has enabled us to introduce a `clear` function that can be used to keep our tests independent of each other. The `beforeEach` block ensures that each test starts from a clean slate.

Summary

This chapter has involved writing many more unit tests than previous chapters. Sometimes, unit tests need to be very detailed, particularly when it comes to testing very specific return values. In *Chapter 8, Creating Matchers to Simplify Tests*, we'll look at ways of reducing the number of tests required.

You've also seen why it's important for unit tests to run independently and how to ensure your SvelteKit route tests clear their data between each test using the `beforeEach` function.

In the next chapter, you'll learn how to extend the current `BirthdayForm` component to handle editing existing birthdays in addition to adding new birthdays.

6

Editing Form Data

The preceding two chapters showed how to build an HTML form to add new birthdays into the *Birthdays* application and how to add server-side validation for that form. This chapter wraps up the form implementation by adding the ability to edit existing birthday information.

Doing this will involve adding Svelte component state to track whether the edit form is in listing or editing mode.

Up to this point, the server has stored data in a plain JavaScript array. We have been using TDD to force the simplest implementation that could possibly work. This chapter brings in a more complex implementation that uses a `Map` object, which we'll do as part of the *Refactor* step as part of the *Red-Green-Refactor* workflow.

This chapter will cover the following key topics:

- Planning the path ahead
- Adding a Playwright test for editing form data
- Evolving the repository to allow ID lookup
- Updating the form action to handle edits
- Updating the list page with a new edit mode

By the end of the chapter, you'll have seen how TDD is used to evolve system design when you increase the functionality of a software system.

Technical requirements

The code for the chapter can be found online at `https://github.com/PacktPublishing/Svelte-with-Test-Driven-Development/tree/main/Chapter06/Start`.

Planning the path ahead

Before we get started with the code, let's do a little upfront design so we have a rough course of action.

The overall goal is to allow every birthday entry in the system to be modified. We'd like to reuse the existing BirthdayForm component so that it can be used for this purpose.

Figure 6.1 shows a diagram of how we could update the system to support this new feature. Each list item will have an **Edit** button that, when clicked, opens up a form for editing. This form replaces the text in the list item with a form. In terms of our components, the Birthday component will be switched to a BirthdayForm component:

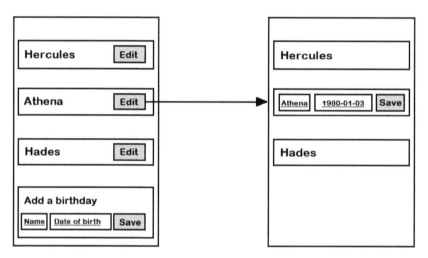

Figure 6.1 – A mockup of editing birthdays

While in this edit mode, it makes sense to hide the form for adding a birthday and also prohibit editing other birthdays, just to ensure that there's only ever one active form on display.

There's one question remaining, and that's how do we let the backend form action know that we're editing a birthday and not adding one?

A straightforward approach to doing this is to add a special id property to each birthday data object. This is a unique value that the server can use to identify each individual object. The id will never change and cannot be edited, whereas the other data items can be changed. And the user never needs to see the id value. Its purpose is simply to enable modification of existing data items.

We can use the standard JavaScript randomUUID function to give us a unique string to create an id for each birthday.

Figure 6.2 shows the various SvelteKit components and functions, together with the important bits of data that are needed to make this work, including a new editing state variable in the page component and the id field used to pick out the birthday for editing:

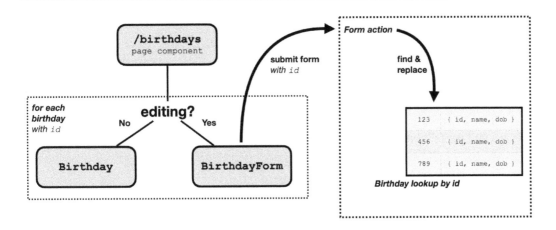

Figure 6.2 – Using the component state and a lookup table to implement edit behavior

Before continuing, it's worth noting that our current birthday repository holds its `birthday` objects in a plain JavaScript array. This is fine for listing and adding new items, but it's not ideal for replacing existing items without updated versions. A better data structure is a `Map` object, which allows us to easily update items based on a key. Since we've already realized we need a fixed `id` value to represent each birthday, we already have a good choice for a key.

That covers our up front design. With a plan in place, it's time for an end-to-end test.

Adding a Playwright test for editing form data

In this section, we'll build the latest Playwright test for our system. Because this test is quite long, we'll build it bit by bit. In *Chapter 7*, *Tidying up Test Suites*, we'll look at how this test script can be shortened.

Let's follow these steps to create the test:

1. In `tests/birthday.test.js`, begin the test with the following code, which loads the application, the `/birthdays` endpoint, and then completes the form to add a new birthday for `Ares`. We have to be careful to find the button specifically with the **Save** name. That's because we'll now have multiple buttons on the page: one named **Save**, and then multiple buttons named **Edit**:

```
test('edits a birthday', async ({ page }) => {
  await page.goto('/birthdays');
  // add a birthday using the form
  await page.getByLabel('Name').fill('Ares');
  await page
    .getByLabel('Date of birth')
    .fill('1985-01-01');
  await page
```

```
    .getByRole('button', { name: 'Save' })
    .click();
});
```

2. Next, add the following command to find the **Edit** button for `Ares`. This uses the special `getByRole('listitem').filter(...)` chain command, which finds an element with the `listitem` role (meaning the `li` elements) that also contains the `'Ares'` text. We then find the **Edit** button within that list item element:

```
await page
  .getByRole('listitem')
  .filter({ hasText: 'Ares' })
  .getByRole('button', { name: 'Edit' })
  .click();
```

3. We now assume that a new form has appeared for editing the birthday information for `Ares`. Continue the test with the following code, which replaces the `Date of birth` field with another value, and then click the **Save** button:

```
await page
  .getByLabel('Date of birth')
  .fill('1995-01-01');
await page
  .getByRole('button', { name: 'Save' })
  .click();
```

4. Finish off the new test with a couple of expectations. We check that the original date of birth no longer appears and that the new date of birth does appear:

```
// check that the original text doesn't appear
await expect(
  page
    .getByRole('listitem')
    .filter({ hasText: 'Ares' })
).not.toContainText('1985-01-01');

// check that the new text does appear
await expect(
  page
    .getByRole('listitem')
    .filter({ hasText: 'Ares' })
).toContainText('1995-01-01');
```

5. Finally, the previous Playwright tests need to be modified. Each test assumed that there was just one button on the page, the **Save** button. But now we're going to have **Edit** buttons too, so we must change the locator calls to `find a button` and change them to be `find a button named Save`. Find all the lines that look like this:

```
await page.getByRole('button').click();
```

And update them to look like this:

```
await page.getByRole('button',
  { name: 'Save' }
).click();
```

That completes the new test. You can see we've already made some design decisions about the new **Edit** buttons and how they operate.

If you run tests now with the `npm test` command, you'll see the new test timeout waiting for the **Edit** button to appear:

```
Test timeout of 30000ms exceeded.

...
waiting for getByRole('listitem').filter({ hasText: 'Ares'
}).getByRole('button', { name: 'Edit' })
```

In the next section, we'll translate that into decisions about the application code.

Evolving the repository to allow ID lookup

It's now time to update our birthday data items to include an `id` field.

Let's start with a new test to check that `id` is present.

1. Start by adding this test into the `src/routes/birthdays/page.server.test.js` file, within the `describe` block named `/birthdays - default action`. It checks that each birthday has a unique `id` field associated with it:

```
it('saves unique ids onto each new birthday', async () => {
  const request = createFormDataRequest({
    name: 'Zeus',
    dob: '2009-02-02'
  });

  await actions.default({ request });
  await actions.default({ request });
```

```
    expect(birthdayRepository.getAll()[0].id).not
    .toEqual(birthdayRepository.getAll()[1].id);
});
```

2. Make that pass in `src/lib/server/birthdayRepository.js`. Start by adding the `import` statement:

```
import { randomUUID } from 'crypto';
```

3. Then update the definition of the `addNew` function:

```
export const addNew = (item) =>
    db.push({ ...item, id: randomUUID() });
```

4. If you run tests now, you'll see that the test passes, but we have a new failure in a different part of the test suite. The `returns a fixture of two items` test is now erroring because of these new `id` fields. We can fix this by using the `expect.objectContaining` constraining function, which is useful for for saying, *I don't care about anything except these properties*. It's a useful tool for reducing the brittleness of tests. Update that test now to read as shown in the following code block:

```
it('returns a fixture of two items', () => {
    const result = load();
    expect(result.birthdays).toEqual([
        expect.objectContaining({
            name: 'Hercules',
            dob: '1994-02-02'
        }),
        expect.objectContaining({
            name: 'Athena',
            dob: '1989-01-01'
        })
    ]);
});
```

5. Now add this next test, which checks that if we send in a request with an `id` property, then we should choose to update the item matching that `id`, rather than adding a new birthday. Notice the use of the `storedId` function, which pulls out the `id` property that was saved into the repository:

```
const storedId = () =>
    birthdayRepository.getAll()[0].id;

it('updates an entry that shares the same id', async () => {
    let request = createFormDataRequest({
        name: 'Zeus',
        dob: '2009-02-02'
```

```
    });

    await actions.default({ request });

    request = createFormDataRequest({
      id: storedId(),
      name: 'Zeus Ex',
      dob: '2007-02-02'
    });
    await actions.default({ request });

    expect(birthdayRepository.getAll()).toHaveLength(1);
    expect(birthdayRepository.getAll()).toContainEqual({
      id: storedId(),
      name: 'Zeus Ex',
      dob: '2007-02-02'
    });
  });
```

6. It's now a great time to refactor our db value to be a Map object rather than an array, as we discussed in the previous section. Doing that refactor will make this new test straightforward. But we don't *refactor* on *Red*. So, begin by skipping the test you just wrote and checking the test suite is *Green*.

```
it.skip('updates an entry that shares the same id', async () =>
{
  ...
});
```

7. In src/lib/server/birthdayRepository.js, replace db, addNew, getAll, and clear with this implementation that uses the Map object:

```
const db = new Map();

export const addNew = (item) => {
  const id = randomUUID();
  db.set(id, { ...item, id });
};

export const getAll = () => Array.from(db.values());

export const clear = () => db.clear();
```

8. Run your tests after this change and make sure they are still *Green*.

> **Refactoring with confidence**
>
> Notice how the presence of your unit tests removes any fear of change when you completely replace the internal data structure. The tests encourage you to make whatever change you need without worrying about unintentional changes in behavior.

All the tests should pass – fantastic!

This section has shown you another example of how we can use TDD to delay complex designs until the point that our unit tests force us. You've seen how we can migrate an important variable from an array to a Map object.

Now let's get on with building the edit feature.

Updating the form action to handle edits

In this section, we'll continue with updating the repository to handle updating birthdays in addition to adding new ones. We'll tackle this in three parts: first, replacing items in the db field, second, guarding against invalid id values, and third, ensuring that id values are passed back in validation errors so that the same birthday can be corrected by the user.

Replacing items in the repository

Let's get started with the test you wrote in the previous section:

1. Un-skip the last test you wrote in the `src/routes/birthdays/page.server.test.js` file. Make sure to run the tests and watch it fail, ensuring you're on *Red*:

    ```
    it('updates an entry that shares the same id', async () => {
      ...
    });
    ```

2. To make that test pass, start by adding a `replace` function to `src/lib/server/birthdayRepository.js`:

    ```
    export const replace = (id, item) =>
      db.set(id, { ...item, id });
    ```

3. Then, import that new function into `src/routes/birthdays/+page.server.js`:

    ```
    import {
      addNew,
      getAll,
      replace
    } from '$lib/server/birthdayRepository.js';
    ```

4. Update the `actions` constant, first by pulling out `id` from the request, and then using that `id` value to switch behavior. If `id` is present, then call the `replace` function; otherwise, call the `addNew` function:

```
export const actions = {
  default: async ({ request }) => {
    const data = await request.formData();
    const id = data.get('id');
    ...
    if (id) {
      replace(id, {
        name,
        dob
      });
    } else {
      addNew({ name, dob });
    }
  }
};
```

5. Re run your tests; you should now be on *Green*.

Next, let's ensure that only valid `id` values are accepted.

Protecting against unknown identifiers

The final validation we need is to make sure that we don't try to update items in the repository that don't exist. Let's begin with a new test context:

1. Still in `src/routes/birthdays/page.server.test.js`, add a new nested `describe` block to the *validation errors* context, as shown in the following code. I've skipped ahead and included *three* tests here since we've solved these kinds of tests before, and we can feel confident about solving them at the same time:

```
describe('when the id is unknown', () => {
  let result;

  beforeEach(async () => {
    const request = createFormDataRequest({
      id: 'unknown',
      name: 'Hercules',
      dob: '2009-01-02'
    });

    result = await actions.default({
      request
```

```
    });
  });

  it('does not save the birthday', () => {
    expect(load().birthdays).not.toContainEqual(
      expect.objectContaining({
        name: 'Hercules',
        dob: 'unknown'
      })
    );
  });

  it('returns a 422', () => {
    expect(result.status).toEqual(422);
  });

  it('returns a useful message', () => {
    expect(result.data.error).toEqual(
      'An unknown ID was provided.'
    );
  });
});
```

2. To make this pass, start by adding a new `has` function to `src/lib/server/birthdayRepository.js`:

    ```
    export const has = (id) => db.has(id);
    ```

3. Then import that into `src/routes/birthdays/+page.server.js`:

    ```
    import {
      addNew,
      getAll,
      replace,
      has
    } from '$lib/server/birthdayRepository.js';
    ```

4. And finally, make use of it by adding a new guard clause.

    ```
    if (id && !has(id)) {
      return fail(422, {
        error: 'An unknown ID was provided.'
      });
    }
    ```

We're almost done with the form action validations, but there's one more thing we need to do.

Updating return values to include identifiers

When a validation error occurs, such as when the name field is empty, we need to ensure the id form value is included in the return error value. That ensures that back in the web browser, the correct edit form can be reopened to allow the user to correct their edits.

Before we launch into the code changes, let's discuss the strategy. This is how the application code will end up looking:

```
if (empty(name)) {
   return fail(422, {
      id,
      dob,
      error: 'Please provide a name.'
   });
}
```

Before you make that change, however, think about how you'll test this. We already have a test that checks the contents of the return value, so one option is to go back and edit this test like this:

```
beforeEach(async () => {
   const request = createFormDataRequest({
      id: '123',
      name: 'Hercules'
   });
});
```

But don't do this.

I find that editing previous tests is generally a bad idea. The reason for that is it can produce tests that end up specifying invalid scenarios that can never happen. The preceding example is indeed an invalid scenario. That's because there's no birthday in the system with an id value of 123. To make it valid, we'd need new test setup instructions that create the birthday with the id value of 123 to ensure the id value is valid.

But if we do that, then we have no test for the original scenario of adding a birthday! Instead, let's create new tests that cover each of the two use cases that can happen: an invalid name or an invalid date of birth when a birthday is being edited.

> **Scenario-based testing**
>
> When you're writing unit tests, always make sure your tests cover valid scenarios. If you're following TDD, that generally means always adding new tests rather than going back to modify existing tests.

Let's begin by adding a new nested context inside the `validation errors` context:

1. Add the following `describe` context with its associated `beforeEach` block, which adds a birthday into the system:

```
describe('when replacing an item', () => {
  beforeEach(async () => {
    let request = createFormDataRequest({
      name: 'Zeus',
      dob: '2009-02-02'
    });
    await actions.default({ request });
  });
});
```

2. Now, add the first test into the context. It attempts to edit the created birthday but has an empty name. The expectation checks that the same `id` value is passed back in the response:

```
it('returns the id when an empty name is provided', async () =>
{
  const request = createFormDataRequest({
    id: storedId(),
    name: '',
    dob: '1982-05-01'
  });

  const result = await actions.default({
    request
  });

  expect(result.data).toContain({ id: storedId() });
});
```

3. To make that pass, include the `id` property in the relevant guard clause:

```
if (empty(name)) {
  return fail(422, {
    id,
    dob,
    error: 'Please provide a name.'
  });
}
```

4. Next, add a test for an invalid date of birth:

```
it('returns the id when an empty date of birth is provided',
async () => {
  const request = createFormDataRequest({
```

```
      id: storedId(),
      name: 'Hercules',
      dob: ''
    });

    const result = await actions.default({
      request
    });

    expect(result.data).toContain({ id: storedId() });
  });
```

5. To make that pass, update the second guard clause, as shown here:

```
if (invalidDob(dob)) {
  return fail(422, {
    id,
    name,
    dob,
    error:
      'Please provide a date of birth in the YYYY-MM-DD format.'
  });
}
```

That completes the changes to the form action.

> **Listening to your tests**
>
> It's very important to listen to your tests. If they are a slog to write and update, that's a sign that either the tests can be improved or the application code design can be improved.

In *Chapter 9, Extracting Logic Out of the Framework*, we'll move validation into the birthday repository, and this will give us a chance to rethink how these tests are structured.

This section has covered a whole bunch of changes: adding repository functionality for replacing items, updating the form action to either add or replace items, adding another guard clause to protect against invalid replacements, and finally, updating the existing guard clauses to return the id value.

Now it's time to update the page component to display `BirthdayForm` in edit mode.

Updating the list page with a new edit mode

In this section, you'll update the page so that it can toggle into an edit mode for a given birthday. That relies on having a hidden form field for the id value.

> **Testing hidden fields**
>
> Testing Library doesn't give us an easy way to query the `hidden` input fields because it generally concerns itself with what is visible to the user, and our `id` field is purposefully designed to be an internal system detail.
>
> Fortunately, we can fall back to the standard **Document Object Model** (**DOM**) Form API to figure this out.
>
> The nature of writing unit tests for frameworks such as SvelteKit means that sometimes you're checking for internal details like this.

Let's start with a new test in a new nested `describe` block:

1. In the `src/routes/birthdays/BirthdayForm.test.js` file, and within the `BirthdayForm` root in the `describe` block, add this new nested `describe` block and test:

```
describe('id field', () => {
  it('contains a hidden field for the id if an id is
  given', () => {
    render(BirthdayForm, { form: { id: '123' } });
    expect(
      document.forms.birthday.elements.id.value
    ).toEqual('123');
  });
});
```

2. To make that pass, update the `BirthdayForm` component (in `src/routes/birthdays/BirthdayForm.svelte`) to include a new hidden field:

```
<form method="post" name="birthday">
  <input type="hidden" name="id" value={form?.id} />
</form>
```

3. Notice how we need optional chaining (with `form?`) to ensure our existing tests, with no `form` prop, continue to work. However, this presents a problem: what is the value of the `id` field if we're not editing but creating? We need another test, which you can add to the same `describe` block:

```
it('does not include the id field if no id is present', () => {
  render(BirthdayForm);
  expect(
    document.forms.birthday.elements.id
  ).not.toBeDefined();
});
```

4. To make that pass, pull up the optional chain into a conditional that wraps the hidden `input` element in the `BirthdayForm` component:

```
<form method="post" name="birthday">
  {#if form?.id}
    <input type="hidden" name="id" value={form.id} />
  {/if}
</form>
```

Okay, that's it for the `BirthdayForm` component itself. Now what about the page component?

Adding a toggle mode to the page

In this section, you'll introduce a component state variable named `editing` that allows us to toggle between *create* and *update* mode.

Let's start by displaying the **Edit** buttons for each of the birthdays listed on the page:

1. In `src/routes/birthdays/page.test.js`, add the following test. Remember that the repository has, by default, two items, so this test allows us to test that *both* have an **Edit** button:

```
it('displays an Edit button for each birthday in the list', ()
=> {
  render(Page, { data: { birthdays } });
  expect(
    screen.queryAllByRole('button', {
      name: 'Edit'
    })
  ).toHaveLength(2);
});
```

2. To make that pass, in `/src/routes/birthdays/+page.svelte`, update each `li` element to contain a new `button` element:

```
<ol>
  {#each data.birthdays as birthday}
    <li>
      <Birthday {...birthday} />
      <button>Edit</button>
    </li>
  {/each}
</ol>
```

3. Next, what happens when we click that button? Let's add a set of tests for checking the behavior when the **Edit** button is pressed. First, add two new imports. The first is for the `beforeEach` function that we're going to use to pull out some common setup for each of our tests. The second is for the `click` function, which will be used to simulate a DOM click event:

```
import {
  describe,
  it,
  expect,
  beforeEach
} from 'vitest';
import { click } from '@testing-library/user-event';
```

4. Then add this new nested `describe` block and test. The `beforeEach` function is used to pull out the *Arrange* portion of the test to avoid having to repeat it in each of the subsequent tests. This code also makes use of a helper function named `firstEditButton` that keeps the tests readable and short:

```
describe('when editing an existing birthday', () => {
  beforeEach(() =>
    render(Page, { data: { birthdays } })
  );

  const firstEditButton = () =>
    screen.queryAllByRole('button', {
      name: 'Edit'
    })[0];

  it('hides the existing birthday information', async
  () => {
    await click(firstEditButton());
    expect(
      screen.queryByText('Hercules')
    ).toBeNull();
  });
});
```

5. To make that pass, start by introducing a new component state variable named `editing` into the page component:

```
<script>
  ...
  let editing = null;
</script>
```

6. When the **Edit** button is pressed, set `editing` to the specific `birthday` object, which is given to us by the `each` construct. We can then wrap the original `Birthday` component in a conditional; if `editing` is equal to the current `birthday` object, then don't show `Birthday`:

```
<ol>
  {#each data.birthdays as birthday}
    <li>
      {#if editing !== birthday}
        <Birthday {...birthday} />
      {/if}
      <button
        on:click={() => (editing = birthday)}>
        Edit</button>
    </li>
  {/each}
</ol>
```

7. Next, we also want to hide the original form for adding the page:

```
it('hides the birthday form for adding new birthdays', async ()
=> {
  await click(firstEditButton());
  expect(
    screen.queryByRole('heading', {
      name: 'Add a new birthday'
    })
  ).toBeNull();
});
```

8. To make that pass, wrap the last bit of the page component in `if`:

```
{#if !editing}
  <h1>Add a new birthday</h1>
  <div>
    <BirthdayForm {form} />
  </div>
{/if}
```

But hang on a second! We're now defining behavior on a static element that we've never tested before: the heading. The Add a new birthday text was something we didn't bother testing. But now that it's an integral part of our test suite, surely we should have a test to prove that it's initially there? (Otherwise, the most straightforward way to get the last test to *Green* would have been to delete the heading.)

In fact, do that now. Go ahead and delete it and watch your test suite happily pass. To bring it back in, we need a failing test:

1. Add this new test right at the top of the test suite:

    ```
    it('displays a heading for "Add a new birthday"', () => {
      render(Page, { data: { birthdays } });
      expect(
        screen.queryByRole('heading', {
          name: 'Add a new birthday'
        })
      ).toBeVisible();
    });
    ```

2. Watch the test fail, and then go ahead and undelete the heading.

3. Onto the next test. This time, let's check that `BirthdayForm` is shown. We can do that by looking for a `Name` field that has the existing name in there (in this case, that's `Hercules`):

    ```
    it('shows the birthday form for editing', async () => {
      await click(firstEditButton());
      expect(
        screen.getByLabelText('Name')
      ).toHaveValue('Hercules');
    });
    ```

4. To make that pass, flesh out the `if` conditional block with a new `:else` block. Notice the order of proceedings swaps around here: if `editing` is equal to `birthday`, then display `BirthdayForm`; otherwise, display `Birthday`:

    ```
    <ol>
      {#each data.birthdays as birthday}
        <li>
          {#if editing == birthday}
            <BirthdayForm form={editing} />
          {:else}
            <Birthday {...birthday} />
          {/if}
          ...
        </li>
      {/each}
    </ol>
    ```

5. Now that we have a **Save** button on the page, shouldn't we hide all the **Edit** buttons? Yes, let's do that:

    ```
    it('hides all the Edit buttons', async () => {
      await click(firstEditButton());
    ```

```
    expect(
      screen.queryByRole('button', {
        name: 'Edit'
      })
    ).toBeNull();
  });
```

6. To make that pass, introduce another `if` block around the button:

    ```
    {#if !editing}
      <button
        on:click={() => (editing = birthday)}>
        Edit</button>
    {/if}
    ```

7. There's one final test left. This is an important one. It checks that if SvelteKit passes us back a `form` object with an `id` value, then we need to immediately start in *edit* mode for that birthday. Since the `id` value is important here, this test includes its own `data` and `form` properties:

    ```
    it('opens the form in editing mode if a form id is passed in',
    () => {
      render(Page, {
        data: {
          birthdays: [
            {
              id: '123',
              name: 'Hercules',
              dob: '1994-02-02'
            }
          ]
        },
        form: {
          id: '123',
          name: 'Hercules',
          dob: 'bad dob',
          error: 'An error'
        }
      });

      expect(
        screen.queryByRole('heading', {
          name: 'Add a new birthday'
        })
      ).toBeNull();
    });
    ```

> **Using factory methods to shorten tests**
>
> In *Chapter 7, Tidying up Test Suites*, you'll create a factory method for birthdays that will shorten this test.

8. The tests allude to the fact that the initial value of editing depends on form. So, update that now to look like this:

    ```
    let editing = form?.id ? form : null;
    ```

9. Then, because we're dealing with different objects, we can no longer use equality based on object identity to match the currently edited birthday. So, update the first if to be the one shown in the following code, which checks id rather than the whole object itself:

    ```
    {#if editing?.id === birthday.id}
      ...
    {/if}
    ```

10. Now, because of this new reliance on the id field, you'll find other tests breaking. Update the birthdays array to include the id values like this:

    ```
    const birthdays = [
      {
        id: '123',
        name: 'Hercules',
        dob: '1994-02-02'
      },
      {
        id: '234',
        name: 'Athena',
        dob: '1989-01-01'
      }
    ];
    ```

After this point, your tests should pass, including your Playwright test.

Figure 6.3 shows what the application looks like if you fire up the dev server (with the npm run dev command) and try to replace an existing birthday with an invalid date:

Figure 6.3 – A validation error when editing a birthday

This section has shown you how you can use the Svelte component state to switch between add and edit modes of a form and how you can test-drive those modifications in both the form component and the page component.

Summary

This chapter has demonstrated how the TDD process works once you have a substantial amount of code in place. In addition, you have seen how we can build feature upon feature using the same *Red-Green-Refactor* workflow that you learned about in *Chapter 2, Introducing the Red-Green-Refactor Workflow*: first, by refactoring the store implementation, and then by introducing Svelte component state.

In the next chapter, we'll stop to look at some of the ways we can simplify the current code base.

Part 2:
Refactoring Tests and
Application Code

Now that you've learned about and practiced the test-driven development workflow, it's time to focus on practices and strategies that will keep your automated tests and application code neat and tidy. The chapters in this part will provide you with guidance on creating elegant and maintainable automated test suites.

This part has the following chapters:

7
Tidying up Test Suites

Have you ever felt frustrated when working with your test suites? They can easily become messy and overgrown, unless you're actively tending to them. In this chapter, we'll look at some of the ways you can keep your test suites tidy.

The techniques you'll use to tidy test suites differ from the techniques you'd use in your application code. Application code requires building abstractions and encapsulating details, with deep layers of connecting objects. However, tests benefit from being shallow, with each test statement having a clear effect.

Another way to think of it is that normal program flow can take many different paths through the code, but test suites have just one flow – they are scripts that run from top to bottom. There is an absence of control logic, such as conditional expressions and loop constructs.

The primary mechanism you have to control complexity in test suites is abstracting functions that hide detail.

This chapter covers the following techniques:

- Using page object models in Playwright tests
- Extracting an action helper
- Extracting a factory method for creating data objects

By the end of the chapter, you'll have learned an array of strategies to cut down on the size of your test suites.

Technical requirements

The code for the chapter can be found online at `https://github.com/PacktPublishing/Svelte-with-Test-Driven-Development/tree/main/Chapter07/Start`.

Using page object models in Playwright tests

A **page object model** is simply a plain JavaScript class that groups up the mechanical actions of navigating a page (locating a field, clicking a button, or filling in a text field) into methods that describe high-level operations that occur within your application (completing a birthday form).

In this section, you'll build a page object model named `BirthdayListPage` that will allow you to rewrite your existing Playwright tests more simply.

Let's get started by adding the new class:

1. Create a new file named `tests/BirthdayListPage.js` and give it the following content. It creates the basic class along with a single method, `goto`, which is used to navigate to the `/birthdays` application URL:

    ```
    export class BirthdayListPage {
      constructor(page) {
        this.page = page;
      }

      async goto() {
        await this.page.goto('/birthdays');
      }
    }
    ```

2. We can already make use of this class in our tests. In `tests/birthdays.test.js`, add the following import at the top of the file:

    ```
    import {
      BirthdayListPage
    } from './BirthdayListPage.js';
    ```

3. Now, update all the tests to use this class, by replacing the direct call to `page.goto` with the indirect call via the `BirthdayListPage` object. For example, consider the following existing test:

    ```
    test('edits a birthday', async ({ page }) => {
      await page.goto('/birthdays');
      ...
    });
    ```

    It should be modified to become this:

    ```
    test('edits a birthday', async ({ page }) => {
      const birthdayListPage = new BirthdayListPage(page);
      await birthdayListPage.goto();
      ...
    });
    ```

4. Now, we'll move on to creating helpers for each of the individual files. Take a look at this original code from the editing test:

```
// add a birthday using the form
await page.getByLabel('Name').fill('Ares');
await page
  .getByLabel('Date of birth')
  .fill('1985-01-01');
await page
  .getByRole('button', { name: 'Save' })
  .click();
```

From this, we can pull helpers called `nameField`, `dateOfBirthField`, and `saveButton`. Now, add them to `BirthdayListPage`, like this:

```
export class BirthdayListPage {
  ...

  dateOfBirthField = () =>
    this.page.getByLabel('Date of birth');

  nameField = () => this.page.getByLabel('Name');

  saveButton = () =>
    this.page.getByRole('button', { name: 'Save' });
}
```

5. Still in `BirthdayLastPage`, you can now roll up these helper methods into a single helper method that performs the whole action, `saveNameAndDateOfBirth`:

```
export class BirthdayListPage {
  ...

  saveNameAndDateOfBirth = async (name, dob) => {
    await this.nameField().fill(name);
    await this.dateOfBirthField().fill(dob);
    await this.saveButton().click();
  };
```

6. The section of code in *step 4* from the original test, which was eight lines of code including the explanatory comment, can now be done in a single function call. The comment is no longer necessary because the method name basically says the same thing. Go ahead and update the test now, as shown here:

```
test('edits a birthday', async ({ page }) => {
  const birthdayListPage = new BirthdayListPage(page);
```

```
await birthdayListPage.goto();

await birthdayListPage.saveNameAndDateOfBirth(
  'Ares',
  '1985-01-01'
);
...
);
```

That completes this section of the test. Now for the next bit, which looks like this:

```
// find the Edit button for that person
await page
  .getByRole('listitem')
  .filter({ hasText: 'Ares' })
  .getByRole('button', { name: 'Edit' })
  .click();
```

For this section, we can repeat the earlier steps to extract an internal helper to locate the desired field, and then extract a second external helper to perform the action. Start by adding a new helper in the BirthdayListPage page object model, named entryFor, that finds the entry for a person's name:

```
entryFor = (name) =>
  this.page
    .getByRole('listitem')
    .filter({ hasText: name });
```

7. Now, use the entryFor method to build another helper, beginEditingFor, which clicks the **Edit** button for that birthday:

```
beginEditingFor = (name) =>
  this.entryFor(name)
    .getByRole('button', { name: 'Edit' })
    .click();
```

8. It's time to remove the original code shown in *step 6* with a single call to this new helper in the page object model. Make the updates shown in the following code block, again getting rid of the comment and reducing six lines down to one:

```
test('edits a birthday', async ({ page }) => {
  const birthdayListPage = new BirthdayListPage(page);
  await birthdayListPage.goto();
  await birthdayListPage.saveNameAndDateOfBirth(
    'Ares',
    '1985-01-01'
  );
```

```
    await birthdayListPage.beginEditingFor('Ares');
    ...
});
```

9. There's one final action within the test that can be updated, which is the action to modify the form values after beginning editing. We don't need to create any new helpers for this action. We simply need to reuse the `saveNameAndDateOfBirth` helper. Go ahead and do that now, like this:

```
test('edits a birthday', async ({ page }) => {
    ...
    await birthdayListPage.beginEditingFor('Ares');
    await birthdayListPage.saveNameAndDateOfBirth(
      'Ares',
      '1995-01-01'
    );
    ...
});
```

10. The last change to make is a change to the expectations. They can be updated to use the `entryFor` helper. Since this is the last change in this section, the listing shows the fully complete test. Make the changes to the expectations as shown here:

```
test('edits a birthday', async ({ page }) => {
    const birthdayListPage = new BirthdayListPage(page);
    await birthdayListPage.goto();
    await birthdayListPage.saveNameAndDateOfBirth(
      'Ares',
      '1985-01-01'
    );
    await birthdayListPage.beginEditingFor('Ares');
    await birthdayListPage.saveNameAndDateOfBirth(
      'Ares',
      '1995-01-01'
    );

    await expect(
      birthdayListPage.entryFor('Ares')
    ).not.toContainText('1985-01-01');

    await expect(
      birthdayListPage.entryFor('Ares')
    ).toContainText('1995-01-01');
});
```

The benefits of introducing the `BirthdayListPage` page object model are clear: the test is more readable, the test data is more prominent (the two changing date of births are now more visible), and any future changes will be quicker to make, simply because the test is shorter.

> **Continuing with the remaining tests**
>
> The other Playwright tests in the repository can also be rewritten using the exact same helpers. These changes aren't shown in this book but are available in the companion repository.

In this section, you saw how to create a Playwright page object model. Next, we'll do something similar with the Vitest unit tests.

Extracting an action helper

This section covers the use of a helper to simplify the *Act* phase of a test.

> **Understanding the Arrange-Act-Assert pattern**
>
> The *Arrange-Act-Assert* pattern is a standard way to describe the order in which unit tests are written.
>
> They start with the *Arrange* phase, which is when the structure under test is primed for work. Any input data is constructed, and any preparatory methods are called that get the system into the right state.
>
> Then, we have the *Act* phase, which invokes the operation that is being checked. Finally, the test ends with the *Assert* phase, which can be one or more expectations (or *assertions*) that verify that the operation did what it was meant to.
>
> Each of these three phases benefits from different strategies to remove duplication.

The *Act* phase is the one that I think benefits least from the removal of duplication. That's because the majority of unit tests you'll write – and all the unit tests in this book – have an action that is triggered by a single method call. It's rare to find a scenario where the action that is being observed requires anything more than a single instruction.

And because of this, I like to ensure the method call is called directly within the unit tests, and not mixed up with any of the *Arrange* phase statements. That being said, there are some occasions when it helps to build an *Act* helper. The call to invoke a SvelteKit form action via the `actions.default` import, is one of these occasions.

There are a couple of reasons why. First, the name `actions.default` is non-descriptive in the context of a unit test suite. Second, the form action's parameter is not trivial – it uses the Form API's `request` object to wrap the form data, which is then packaged into a SvelteKit `RequestEvent`-like object. This needs to be done in every single test. What we care about are the values within the form data, not the plumbing around it.

In the `src/routes/birthdays/page.server.test.js` file, you'll see the following pattern repeated many times:

```
const request = createFormDataRequest({
  // ... the form data object ...
});

await actions.default({ request });
```

You can consider the request statement part of the setup. It is required every single time the form action is called. There is no way to call the form action without doing the form data dance.

So, let's create a helper that wraps this behavior. We'll call it `performFormAction`, which makes it clear what's happening in the test.

Let's begin:

1. In `src/routes/birthdays/page.server.test.js`, add the following function definition to the top of the `/birthdays - default action` context:

    ```
    const performFormAction = (formData) =>
      actions.default({
        request: createFormDataRequest(formData)
      });
    ```

2. In each test, look for the pattern described in the preceding code snippet – calling `createFormDataRequest` and then the imported `actions.default` function – and replace each instance with a call to `performFormAction`. The following is an example from one of the tests:

    ```
    it('adds a new birthday into the list', async () => {
      await performFormAction({
        name: 'Zeus',
        dob: '2009-02-02'
      });

      expect(birthdayStore.getAll()).toContainEqual(
        expect.objectContaining({
          name: 'Zeus',
          dob: '2009-02-02'
        });
      });
    });
    ```

Make sure you rerun all your tests once you've made that change in all of them in the test suite. In the next section, we'll continue with a look at simplifying the *Arrange* section of the test suite.

Extracting a factory method for creating data objects

It's time to simplify the *Arrange* phase of the tests using a factory method named `createBirthday`.

The last section mentioned how each of the *Arrange-Act-Assert* phases needs a different treatment for simplification. A key method for the *Arrange* phase is the use of factories. You already created one of those in *Chapter 4, Saving Form Data*. That was the `createFormDataRequest` method that you used in the preceding section.

> **Using test factories to hide irrelevant data**
>
> Factory methods help you generate supporting objects in the shortest amount of code possible. One way they do that is by setting default values for object properties so that you don't need to specify them. You're then free to override those defaults in each individual test.
>
> Hiding necessary but irrelevant data is a key method for keeping unit tests succinct and clear.

Our birthday objects have a very simple structure, with just three fields – `name`, `dob`, and `id`. Of these three, `name` and `dob` are set frequently and the `id` field infrequently. Also, each of the individual fields has a unique shape of data – a name looks very different from a date, and very different from a **universally unique identifier** (**UUID**).

With that in mind, the upcoming `createBirthday` helper requires both `name` and `dob` but leaves `id` as an extra field that can sometimes be specified. Those `name` and `dob` values are given as positional parameters – meaning they are identified by position and not by name – because it's obvious which is which. That saves space on the page.

It might not seem important, but when you are writing software for maintainability, every single word must prove its worth.

Here's an example of how this looks. Note how `id` is specified differently, due to being rarely used:

```
createBirthday('Zeus Ex', '2007-02-02', { id: storedId() })
```

Let's begin:

1. Create a new file named `src/factories/birthday.js` and give it the following content:

    ```
    export const createBirthday = (
      name,
      dob,
      extra = {}
    ) => ({ name, dob, ...extra });
    ```

2. Open the `src/routes/birthdays/Birthday.test.js` file and import the new helper:

```
import {
  createBirthday
} from src/factories/birthday.js';
```

3. Next, find all the `render` calls that use the `exampleBirthday` object. They look like this:

```
render(Birthday, {
  ...exampleBirthday,
  name: 'Hercules'
});
```

Update them to use the new helper, like this:

```
render(
  Birthday,
  createBirthday('Hercules', '1996-03-03')
);
```

4. Then, in `src/routes/birthdays/page.server.test.js`, add the `createBirthday` import:

```
import {
  createBirthday
} from 'src/factories/birthday.js';
```

5. Find all the calls to `performFormAction` that you updated in the previous section. They'll look something like this:

```
await performFormAction({
  name: 'Zeus',
  dob: '2009-02-02'
});
```

Update them to use the `createBirthday` helper, shown here:

```
await performFormAction(
  createBirthday('Zeus', '2009-02-02')
);
```

There are a couple of tests where the preceding change isn't straightforward. In the *saves unique ids one each new birthday* test, you can save the created birthday in the `request` object, and then pass that into `performFormAction` twice, as shown in the following code:

```
it('saves unique ids onto each new birthday', async () => {
  const request = createBirthday(
    'Zeus',
    '2009-02-02'
```

```
  );
  await performFormAction(request);
  await performFormAction(request);

  expect(birthdayStore.getAll()[0].id).not.toEqual(
    birthdayStore.getAll()[1].id
  );
});
```

The *updates an entrythat shares the same id* test needs a specific id passed into the second invocation. Note how the factory method is structured in such a way that uncommon information needs to be named, such as the id field:

```
it('updates an entry that shares the same id', async () => {
  await performFormAction(
    createBirthday('Zeus', '2009-02-02')
  );

  await performFormAction(
    createBirthday('Zeus Ex', '2007-02-02', { id:
      storedId() })
  );

  expect(birthdayStore.getAll()).toHaveLength(1);
  expect(birthdayStore.getAll()).toContainEqual({
    id,
    name: 'Zeus Ex',
    dob: '2007-02-02'
  });
});
```

6. For the final test suite, in src/routes/birthdays/page.test.js, the birthdays array can be updated to use two calls to createBirthday, as shown here:

```
const birthdays = [
  createBirthday('Hercules', '1994-02-02', {
    id: '123'
  }),
  createBirthday('Athena', '1989-01-01', {
    id: '234'
  })
];
```

7. Finally, update the test shown here so that it uses the `createBirthday` helper directly in the `render` call for both the `birthdays` prop value and the `form` prop value:

```
it('displays all the birthdays passed to it', () => {
  render(Page, {
    data: {
      birthdays: [
        createBirthday('Hercules', '1994-02-02', {
        id: '123'
        })
      ]
    },
    form: {
      ...createBirthday('Hercules', 'bad dob', {
      id: '123'
      }),
      error: 'An error'
    }
  });
});
```

That completes the use of `createBirthday`. Make sure to rerun your tests to ensure that everything is still green.

You've now learned how a test factory method can be used to simplify and bring clarity to your unit tests.

Summary

This chapter has shown you three techniques to shorten your test suites: page object models for Playwright end-to-end tests, action helpers for Vitest unit tests, and factory methods. Keeping test suites clear and meaningful is key to keeping them easily maintainable.

In this next chapter, we'll look at a more involved way of reducing unit test code – writing your own custom matchers.

8

Creating Matchers
to Simplify Tests

This chapter introduces another method for simplifying tests: building custom matchers. Most of the time, it makes sense to stick to the built-in matchers. For instance, the powerful combination of the `toEqual` matcher with the `expect.objectContaining` and `expect.arrayContaining` functions make it easy to build expressive expectations.

But sometimes it makes sense to build a matcher that can scoop up a number of different checks into one single check. This not only shortens tests but can make them more readable, too.

In *Chapter 5*, *Validating Form Data*, each of the form validation rules was tested by a `describe` context with four tests, like this:

```
describe('when the date of birth is in the wrong format')
  it('does not save the birthday', ...)
  it('returns a 422', ...)
  it('returns a useful message', ...)
  it('returns the other data back including the incorrect
      value', ...)
});
```

Since all the validation rules have the same format, it seems like a good candidate for abstracting some shared code. The matcher we'll create will scoop three of these tests into a custom matcher – the `toBeUnprocessableEntity` matcher – that can be used to replace them all with a single test:

```
it('returns a complete error response', async () => {
  const result = await performFormAction(
    createBirthday('Hercules', 'unknown')
  );

  expect(result).toBeUnprocessableEntity({
    error:
```

```
        'Please provide a date of birth in the YYYY-MM-DD
         format.',
      name: 'Hercules',
      dob: 'unknown'
    });
  });
```

There's one final important point: the custom matcher requires its own set of unit tests. That's so you can be sure that the matcher does the right thing: it passes when it's meant to pass, and it fails when it's meant to fail. Just like how you want to be sure that your application code does the right thing.

> **Testing test code**
> The general rule I have is this: if your code contains any kind of control structure or branching logic, such as `if` statements or loop constructs, then it needs tests.

This chapter covers the following:

- Test-driving the pass or failure of an expectation
- Providing extra information in failure messages
- Implementing the negated matcher
- Updating existing tests to use the matcher

By the end of the chapter, you'll understand how to build a matcher and how to write tests for it.

Technical requirements

The code for the chapter can be found online at `https://github.com/PacktPublishing/Svelte-with-Test-Driven-Development/tree/main/Chapter08/Start`.

Test-driving the pass or failure of an expectation

In this section, you'll build the basic functionality of the `toBeUnprocessableEntity` matcher, ensuring that it will correctly pass or fail your test. But first, we'll look at the structure of a matcher and then the approach to unit testing matchers.

Understanding matcher structure

Let's look at the basic structure of a matcher and how we can test it:

```
export function toTestSomething(received, expected) {
  const pass = ...
```

```
   const message = () => "..."
   return {
    pass,
    message
   };
  }
```

The `received` parameter value is the object passed to the `expect` call. The `expected` value is the value passed to the matcher. So, in the example from the introduction, the result is the received object, and the object containing the `error`, `name`, and `dob` properties is the expected object.

The `return` value has two important properties: `pass` and `message`. The `pass` boolean should be `true` if your matcher passes the check, and `false` otherwise. However, for a negated matcher, the opposite happens: a `true` value for `pass` means that the expectation fails.

The `message` property is a function that returns a string. This string is what the test runner displays in the event that your test fails. The contents of the string should be enough for the developer to pinpoint what error occurs. The property itself is defined as a function so that it can be lazily evaluated: there's no point running this code if the test passes.

Unlike other code samples in this book, the matcher function will be defined using the standard `function` keyword. This means it gains access to the `this` bound variable.

Vitest primes `this` with a number of useful utility functions that the matcher can use. We'll use a couple of them in this chapter: `this.equals` and `this.utils.diff`. Another useful property is `this.isNot`, which is `true` if your matcher was invoked in its negated form.

Testing a matcher

There are a couple of ways to test a matcher. One way is to test the function return values, as you would with any other function. The difficulty with this approach is that you'll need to set up the `this` variable, and that's not straightforward.

Another approach, and the approach we'll use this in this chapter, is to use the `toThrowError` matcher to wrap the matcher under test, like this:

```
expect(() =>
  expect(response).toBeUnprocessableEntity()
).toThrowError(
  'Expected 422 status code but got 500'
);
```

The `toThrowError` matcher takes a function as the parameter to expect; this is then executed within a `try` block. The caught `Error` object then has its `message` value checked against the expected value.

For this approach to work, we'll need to ensure `toBeUnprocessableEntity` is registered with the Vitest test runner. We can do that with the `beforeAll` function that runs once at the very beginning test suite.

With all that knowledge, we're ready to begin writing the matcher.

Writing the toBeUnprocessableEntity matcher

Let's get started with the test suite:

1. Create a new file named `src/matchers/toBeUnprocessableEntity.test.js`, and start with the following imports. They include all the Vitest imports, which we'll use in the next step. We'll also import the `fail` SvelteKit function, which we'll use in our tests:

    ```
    import {
      describe,
      it,
      expect,
      beforeAll
    } from 'vitest';
    import { fail } from '@sveltejs/kit';
    import {
      toBeUnprocessableEntity
    } from './toBeUnprocessableEntity.js';
    ```

2. Next, create a new `describe` block with a `beforeAll` block at the start. This ensures that the new matcher is registered before our tests run. This only needs to be done once:

    ```
    describe('toBeUnprocessableEntity', () => {
      beforeAll(() => {
        expect.extend({ toBeUnprocessableEntity });
      });
    });
    ```

3. Our first test will cause the expectation to fail. Add the following test code, which creates a failure reason with a `500` error code rather than a `422`, and then use the `toThrowError` matcher to check that the expectation fails:

    ```
    it('throws if the status is not 422', () => {
      const response = fail(500);
      expect(() =>
        expect(response).toBeUnprocessableEntity()
      ).toThrowError();
    });
    ```

4. To make that test pass, all we need to do is build a matcher that returns a `pass` value of `false`. Create a new file named `src/matchers/toBeUnprocessableEntity.js` with the following content. As mentioned previously, this uses the `function` keyword syntax so that we gain access to Vitest's matcher utility functions that are attached to the `this` variable:

```
export function toBeUnprocessableEntity(
  received, expected
) {
  return { pass: false };
}
```

5. With the first test passing, add the second. This one checks the opposite – that the matcher does not throw if the response has a `422` error code:

```
it('does not throw if the status is 422', () => {
  const response = fail(422);
  expect(() =>
    expect(response).toBeUnprocessableEntity()
  ).not.toThrowError();
});
```

6. To make that pass, wrap the original code in a conditional so that it becomes a guard clause, and if that condition isn't met, then return a `pass` value of `true`, as shown:

```
export function toBeUnprocessableEntity(
  received, expected
) {
  if (received.status !== 422) {
    return { pass: false };
  }

  return { pass: true };
}
```

7. If a failure occurs, we want the test runner to display a helpful message about why the expectation failed. To do that, you can pass a string value to the `toThrowError` matcher that defines the error message. This is what the Vitest test runner will display on the screen. Add the following test:

```
it('returns a message that includes the actual error code', ()
=> {
  const response = fail(500);
  expect(() =>
    expect(response).toBeUnprocessableEntity()
  ).toThrowError(
    'Expected 422 status code but got 500'
```

```
      );
    });
```

8.   Making that pass involves sending back the `message` property. The value of this property is a function that is only invoked if the test fails. It's a form of lazy evaluation, allowing the test runner to avoid doing unnecessary work. Update the guard clause to include the `message` property, as shown:

```
if (received.status !== 422) {
  return {
    pass: false,
    message: () =>
      `Expected 422 status code but got
        ${received.status}`
  };
}
```

9.   Next, we also need to check the `response` body. In our application code, any `422` result returns an `error` property along with the original form values. We want the matcher to fail the test if the actual response doesn't match the expected value:

```
it('throws error if the provided object does not match', () => {
  const response = fail(422, { a: 'b' });
  expect(() =>
    expect(response).toBeUnprocessableEntity({
      c: 'd'
    })
  ).toThrowError();
});
```

10.   To make that pass, all we need is to add a very simple second guard clause. If an argument is passed to the matcher, then we fail the test. This implementation isn't even close to a correct implementation, but it's enough to make the test pass. We'll need to triangulate with more tests. But for now, you can start with this code:

```
export function toBeUnprocessableEntity(
  received,
  expected
) {
  if (received.status !== 422) {
    ...
  }

  if (expected) {
    return {
```

```
      pass: false
    };
  }


  ...

}
```

11. The next test is very similar, but this time, the two response bodies *do* match. This case shouldn't cause a failure error:

```
it('does not throw error if the provided object does match', ()
=> {
  const response = fail(422, { a: 'b' });
  expect(() =>
    expect(response).toBeUnprocessableEntity({
      a: 'b'
    })
  ).not.toThrowError();
});
```

12. Update the second guard clause to use the `this.equals` function to perform a deep equality check on the `received.data` value and the `expected` parameter. This is enough to make the test pass:

```
export function toBeUnprocessableEntity(
  received,
  expected
) {
  if (received.status !== 422) {
    ...
  }


  if (!this.equals(received.data, expected)) {
    return {
      pass: false
    };
  }


  ...
};
```

13. The final test is a check that partial objects match:

```
it('does not throw error if the provide object is a partial
match', () => {
  const response = fail(422, { a: 'b', c: 'd' });
  expect(() =>
    expect(response).toBeUnprocessableEntity({
      a: 'b'
    })
  ).not.toThrowError();
});
```

14. To make that pass, we will use the `expect.objectContaining` constraint function, which can be passed into the call to `this.equals`. Start by importing the `expect` object at the top of the test file:

```
import { expect } from 'vitest';
```

15. Then, update the guard class to wrap the `expected` value in a call to `expect.objectContaining`, as shown:

```
if (
  !this.equals(
    received.data,
    expect.objectContaining(expected)
  )
) {
  ...
}
```

16. Finally, if you run tests now, you'll find the very first test fails because the value of `expected` is `undefined`, and `expect.objectContaining` doesn't like that. To fix the issue, set a default value for the `expected` argument, like this:

```
export function toBeUnprocessableEntity(
  received,
  expected = {}
) {
  ...
}
```

You've now seen how to test-drive a matcher function. The next section focuses on improving the error messages that are displayed when a failure occurs.

Providing extra information in failure messages

This section improves the detailed information that is presented to the developer when a test fails. The purpose of this extra information is to help pinpoint the issue with the application code so that the developer isn't left scratching their head about what went wrong.

Let's begin:

1. Add the next test, which checks that a basic message is shown when the response bodies do not match:

```
it('returns a message if the provided object does not match', ()
=> {
  const response = fail(422, { a: 'b' });
  expect(() =>
    expect(response).toBeUnprocessableEntity({
      c: 'd'
    })
  ).toThrowError(/Response body was not equal/);
});
```

2. To make that pass, add the `message` property to the second guard clause `return` value. We'll expand on this in the next test:

```
if (!this.equals(...)) {
  return {
    pass: false,
    message: () => 'Response body was not equal'
  };
}
```

3. Vitest includes a built-in object `diff` helper that will print out a colorful diff. Colors are added into the text string using ANSI color codes, which the Terminal will decipher and use to switch on and off colors. The presence of these codes means that checking the text content within the `toThrowError` matcher is not straightforward. The following test shows a pragmatic way of checking the same thing in a simpler way, by checking that both the c and a properties appear somewhere in the output:

```
it('includes a diff if the provided object does not match', ()
=> {
  const response = fail(422, { a: 'b' });
  expect(() =>
    expect(response).toBeUnprocessableEntity({
      c: 'd'
    })
```

```
    ).toThrowError('c:');
    expect(() =>
      expect(response).toBeUnprocessableEntity({
        c: 'd'
      })
    ).toThrowError('a:');
  });
```

4. To make that pass, we'll append the diff onto the end of message that we're already printing. First, import the EOL constant from Node.js's os module, which gives us the current platform's line-ending:

    ```
    import { EOL } from 'os';
    ```

5. In the matcher code, update the second guard clause's message property to use the this. utils.diff function to print the diff of the expected and received.data objects:

    ```
    return {
      pass: false,
      message: () =>
        `Response body was not equal:` + EOL +
        this.utils.diff(expected, received.data)
    };
    ```

That completes the display of detailed error information. We'll finish off our matcher in the next section by ensuring it works nicely when used in a negated sense.

Implementing the negated matcher

Negating a matcher is a tricky business, mainly because negated matchers can have confusing meanings. For example, what does the following expectation mean?

```
expect(result).not.toBeUnprocessableEntity({
  error: 'An unknown ID was provided.'
});
```

Presumably, it should fail if the response is 422 and the response body matches the object provided. But should it also fail if the response is, say, a 500 or 200 response? If that was what was expected, wouldn't it be enough to write this?

```
expect(result).not.toBeUnprocessableEntity();
```

I find that when writing matchers for domain-specific ideas, negated matchers are best avoided, or at least restricted in their use. However, to show how it's done, let's carry on with the matcher.

When we negate the matcher, the Vitest test runner will fail the test if the matcher returns a `pass` value of `true`. We have exactly one scenario where this occurs, as all our guard clauses return a `pass` value of `false`. So, all these remaining tests simply check the `message` property in this case.

Let's start by creating a nested `describe` block:

1. Add a nested `describe` block named simply `not`, and add the first test:

    ```
    describe('not', () => {
      it('returns a message if the status is 422 with the
      same body', () => {
        const response = fail(422, { a: 'b' });
        expect(() =>
          expect(response).not.toBeUnprocessableEntity({
            a: 'b'
          })
        ).toThrowError(
          /Expected non-422 status code but got 422/
        );
      });
    });
    ```

2. To make that pass, head to the bottom of the matcher and add the basic `message` property value to the last `return` value in the function, as shown:

    ```
    return {
      pass: true,
      message: () => 'Expected non-422 status code but got 422'
    };
    ```

3. We can improve upon that by ensuring that the actual `response` body is returned in the message. Add the next test:

    ```
    it('includes with the received response body in the message', ()
    => {
      const response = fail(422, { a: 'b' });
      expect(() =>
        expect(response).not.toBeUnprocessableEntity({
          a: 'b'
        })
      ).toThrowError(/"a": "b"/);
    });
    ```

4. To make that pass, you can make use of the `this.utils.stringify` utility function, which does all the hard work for you:

    ```
    return {
      pass: true,
    ```

```
    message: () =>
      `Expected non-422 status code but got 422 with
        body:` + EOL +
      this.utils.stringify(received.data)
};
```

5. Finally, we need to be careful about the case when no expected object is passed in. When this happens, the actual body isn't relevant for the developer since, by omitting it from the expectation, they have expressed that they aren't interested in it:

```
it('returns a negated message for a non-422 status with no
body', () => {
  const response = fail(422);
  expect(() =>
    expect(response).not.toBeUnprocessableEntity()
  ).toThrowError(
    'Expected non-422 status code but got 422'
  );
});
```

6. To make that pass, add a third guard clause, as shown:

```
if (!received.data) {
  return {
    pass: true,
    message: () =>
      'Expected non-422 status code but got 422'
  };
}
```

You've now test-driven a complete matcher, with useful error messages and support for the negated form. Next, it's time to make use of it in our existing test suites.

Updating existing tests to use the matcher

In this final section, we'll use the matcher we've just built to simplify the form validation error test suite. Let's get started:

1. First, register the matcher for our test runs by adding an import statement and call to expect. extend in the src/vitest/registerMatchers.js file:

```
...

import {
  toBeUnprocessableEntity
} from './src/matchers/toBeUnprocessableEntity.js';
```

```
...
expect.extend({ toBeUnprocessableEntity });
```

2. Then, in `src/routes/birthdays/page.server.test.js`, find the nested `describe` block with the description when the name is not provided. It contains four tests. Leave the first one in place, and replace the last three tests with the following test:

```
describe('when the name is not provided', () => {
  ...
  it('does not save the birthday', ...);

  it('returns a complete error response', () => {
    expect(result).toBeUnprocessableEntity({
      error: 'Please provide a name.',
      dob: '2009-02-02'
    });
  });
});
```

3. Then, do the same for the nested `describe` block with the description when the date of birth is in the wrong format, replacing the last three tests with the test shown:

```
describe('when the date of birth is in the wrong format', () =>
{
  ...
  it('does not save the birthday', ...);

  it('returns a complete error response', () => {
    expect(result).toBeUnprocessableEntity({
      error:
        'Please provide a date of birth in the YYYY-
          MM-DD format.',
      name: 'Hercules',
      dob: 'unknown'
    });
  });
});
```

4. Do exactly the same thing with the when the id is unknown context:

```
describe('when the id is unknown', () => {
  ...
  it('does not save the birthday', ...);
```

```
it('returns a complete error message', () => {
  expect(result).toBeUnprocessableEntity({
    error: 'An unknown ID was provided.'
  });
});
});
```

5. Next, there are a couple of tests specifically for ensuring id is returned. Update the expectations for them both, as shown:

```
it('returns the id when an empty name is provided', async () =>
{
  ...
  expect(result).toBeUnprocessableEntity({
    id: storedId()
  });
});
```

```
...
```

```
it('returns the id when an empty date of birth is provided',
async () => {
  ...
  expect(result).toBeUnprocessableEntity({
    id: storedId()
  });
});
```

And that completes the changes. Make sure to run all tests and check that everything is passing. Take a step back and look at how much clearer and simpler your tests have become.

Summary

This chapter has shown you how to build a custom matcher to simplify your test expectations. It also discussed the importance of test-driving matcher code.

Your unit test files act as a specification of your software. It's imperative that these files are clear and concise so that the specifications are clear. Sometimes, writing custom matchers can help you achieve that clarity.

Why do we test-drive matcher implementations? Because almost all matchers have branching logic – sometimes they'll pass and sometimes they'll fail – and you want to be sure that the right branches are used at the right times.

In the next chapter, we'll switch back to refactoring our application code, with the intention of improving its testability.

9

Extracting Logic Out of the Framework

An important property of maintainable software is its **testability**. This is the idea that all parts of the application should be straightforward to test. More specifically, the design of the application code should make it easy to write automated unit tests.

In this chapter, we'll look at one technique for improving testability: moving domain logic out of the framework and into plain JavaScript. Plain JavaScript code is simpler to test because there are no complex framework objects that interact with your code.

The following diagram shows how to think about a SvelteKit code base in this way.

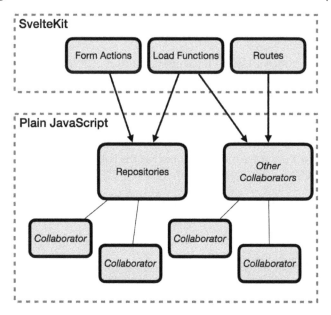

Figure 9.1 – Keeping application code outside of framework components to aid testability

In *Chapter 7, Tidying up Test Suites*, we took a step toward moving the storage of birthday data items into a `birthdayRepository` module. We'll continue that process by pushing data validation out of the SvelteKit form action and into `birthdayRepository` That means we can test complex validation rules without having to set up the complex SvelteKit form request objects, and without having to test the form response objects either.

And since the repository has no asynchronous behavior, the moved tests no longer need to be littered with `async` and `await` keywords.

The following topics are covered in this chapter:

- Migrating tests with a test to-do list
- Porting tests from the form action
- Duplicating form validation behavior in the repository
- Extracting common methods

By the end of the chapter, you'll have used a test-driven approach to move domain logic out of the framework.

Technical requirements

The code for the chapter can be found online at `https://github.com/PacktPublishing/Svelte-with-Test-Driven-Development/tree/main/Chapter09/Start`.

Migrating tests with a test todo list

The task at hand is moving the validation logic out of the SvelteKit form action we completed in *Chapter 5, Validating Form Data*, and into the `birthdayRepository` module. And in this section, we'll plan that task using a new technique.

You might remember that the `birthdayRepository` module already exists but has no tests. That's a situation that we often find ourselves in when we extract modules during refactoring. And it's often perfectly okay to leave these modules untested. The issue comes when we want to modify the behavior of these modules: where do we add the tests?

There's no clear answer to that, but in this case, we'll use the opportunity to duplicate all the tests from the form action in the `birthdayRepository` module, in addition to adding some new tests too.

> **Deleting tests in the original location**
>
> We won't delete the original tests, but that is something you should consider doing so that you're not at risk of over-testing. (The only thing worse than over-testing is under-testing!)

There's a special modifier of the it test function that can be used for planning a test suite: the it.todo modifier. As a form of up-front planning, it's useful when you already have a concrete idea of the tests you'll need in a test suite.

The birthdayRepository module has two exported functions that we're interested in testing: the addNew and replace functions. We will split the existing form action tests between the two new functions. The tests for validation errors will need to be duplicated for both functions. In this way, each function will be fully specified.

Go ahead and create the src/lib/server/birthdayRepository.test.js file with the following content. This gets all the imports in place and primes the birthdayRepository test suite with a call to clear so that each test starts from a blank slate.

There's also a definition of storedId – we can use the same technique for verifying data that we used in the form action tests. And we also add an empty test for checking the initial state:

```
import { describe, it, expect, beforeEach } from 'vitest';
import {
  createBirthday
} from 'src/factories/birthday.js';
import {
  addNew, clear, getAll, replace
} from './birthdayRepository.js';

describe('birthdayRepository', () => {
  beforeEach(clear);

  const storedId = () => getAll()[0].id;

  it.todo('is initially empty');
});
```

Now, add a nested describe block for the addNew function. This takes the original test descriptions from the src/routes/birthdays/page.server.test.js file and morphs them into a more appropriate form:

```
describe('addNew', () => {
  it.todo('adds a new birthday into the list');
  it.todo('saves unique ids onto each new birthday');
  it.todo('returns the added birthday with its id');
  describe('validation errors', () => {
    describe.todo('when the name is not provided');
    describe.todo(
      'when the date of birth in the right format'
    );
```

```
    });
  });
```

It's time to look at the tests for the `replace` function. You'll see that the validation errors are repeated from the `addNew` context. That highlights a difference when splitting a single `entrypoint` (the form action) into two (the `addNew` and `replace` functions):

```
describe('replace', () => {
  it.todo('updates an entry that shares the same id');
  it.todo('returns the updated birthday');

  describe('validation errors', () => {
    describe.todo('when the name is not provided');
    describe.todo(
      'when the date of birth in the right format'
    );
    it.todo(
      'returns the id when an empty date of birth is
        provided'
    );
  });
});
```

The plan is complete. The remaining sections in this chapter will complete the test suite, starting with the *happy path* tests, which already pass, and then going back to complete the validation errors.

Porting tests from the form action

In this section, we'll write out tests for the behavior that already exists in the `birthdayRepository` module, together with ensuring that the functions return values for the form action to reuse.

The `src/lib/server/birthdayRepository.js` file already contains the working code that you last touched on in *Chapter 6, Editing Form Data*. Here's a reminder:

```
import { randomUUID } from 'crypto';

const db = new Map();

export const addNew = (item) => {
  const id = randomUUID();
  db.set(id, { ...item, id });
};

export const getAll = () => Array.from(db.values());
```

```
export const clear = () => db.clear();

export const replace = (id, item) =>
  db.set(id, { ...item, id });

export const has = (id) => db.has(id);
```

Most of this functionality is tested by way of the form action. We need to add tests and then double-check that they work.

Always requiring a failing test

When porting tests, you'll be writing tests that already pass. You skip the *Red* step and pass directly to *Green*. However, it's still important to verify that your tests check the correct thing, and the way to do that is to delete or comment out the application code under test so that you can see the test fail.

Let's start on that now:

1. In `src/lib/server/birthdayRepository.test.js`, remove the `.todo` modifier from the first test, and add the following test content:

    ```
    it('is initially empty', () => {
      expect(getAll()).toHaveLength(0);
    });
    ```

2. You'll see that the test already passed. Verify that it tests the right thing by replacing the `getAll` implementation with a `null` return value, and then re-run the test to check that it's red. An easy way to do this is to comment out the rest of the line, like this:

    ```
    export const getAll = () =>
      null; //Array.from(db.values());
    ```

3. After checking that the test fails, bring the original implementation back and verify that it's green.

4. Fill out the body of the next test, as shown in the following code. This is now a simpler test than the form action test we're porting, for a couple of reasons. First, there's no longer any asynchronous behavior, and second, we use a single factory method of `createBirthday` and avoid the more complex `performFormAction` helper method:

    ```
    describe('addNew', () => {
      it('adds a new birthday into the list', () => {
        addNew(createBirthday('Zeus', '2009-02-02'));
        expect(getAll()).toContainEqual(
          expect.objectContaining({
    ```

```
          name: 'Zeus',
          dob: '2009-02-02'
        })
      );
    });
  });
```

5. Although this will already pass, it's important to check that it's red. You can do that by using the same technique of commenting out the relevant line of code, like this:

    ```
    export const addNew = (item) => {
      const id = randomUUID();
      //db.set(id, { ...item, id });
    };
    ```

6. After verifying that the test fails, undo the commented code and get the test back to green.

7. Next, fill out the third test:

    ```
    it('saves unique ids onto each new birthday', () => {
      const birthday = createBirthday(
        'Zeus',
        '2009-02-02'
      );
      addNew(birthday);
      addNew(birthday);

      expect(getAll()[0].id).not.toEqual(
        getAll()[1].id
      );
    });
    ```

8. To verify that, you can comment out the id value:

    ```
    export const addNew = (item) => {
      const id = null; //randomUUID();
      db.set(id, { ...item, id });
    };
    ```

9. Now, we come on to the test for new behavior, checking that the object is returned together with its new id property. This uses the storedId function defined at the top of the test suite:

    ```
    it('returns the added birthday with its id', () => {
      expect(
        addNew(createBirthday('Zeus', '2009-02-02'))
      ).toEqual({
    ```

```
      id: storedId(),
      name: 'Zeus',
      dob: '2009-02-02'
    });
  });
```

10. To make that pass, introduce a variable named `itemWithId` and return it:

```
export const addNew = (item) => {
  ...
  const itemWithId = { ...item, id };
  db.set(id, itemWithId);
  return itemWithId;
};
```

11. Now, let's move on to the `replace` tests. We'll start with the migration of the `beforeEach` block and the `storedId` method:

```
describe('replace', () => {
  beforeEach(() =>
    addNew(createBirthday('Hercules', '1991-05-06'))
  );

  const storedId = () => getAll()[0].id;
  ...
});
```

12. Then, we'll move on to the first test for the `replace` function. You can verify that in the same way you verified the first test for `getAll`, by giving it a `null` implementation:

```
it('updates an entry that shares the same id', () => {
  replace(
    storedId(),
    createBirthday('Zeus Ex', '2007-02-02')
  );
  expect(getAll()).toHaveLength(1);
  expect(getAll()).toContainEqual({
    id: storedId(),
    name: 'Zeus Ex',
    dob: '2007-02-02'
  });
});
```

13. The final test in this section ensures that we returned the updated item:

```
it('returns the updated birthday', () => {
  expect(
    replace(
      storedId(),
      createBirthday('Zeus Ex', '2007-02-02')
    )
  ).toEqual({
    id: storedId(),
    name: 'Zeus Ex',
    dob: '2007-02-02'
  });
});
```

14. To make that pass, make exactly the same change that you made in the addNew function:

```
export const replace = (id, item) => {
  ...
  const itemWithId = { ...item, id };
  db.set(id, itemWithId);
  return itemWithId;
};
```

That's all the tests that prove the existing behavior. In the next section, we'll need to port across the implementation in addition to the test cases.

Duplicating form validation behavior in the repository

In this section, we'll continue porting across tests from the src/routes/birthdays/page.
server.test.js file, but now we're going to duplicate the validation behavior within the form
action itself.

> **Repetition as a design signal**
>
> The following steps contain a fair amount of repetition. First, the tests are very similar to tests
> you've already written in the form action. Second, the same checks are repeated for both the
> addNew and replace functions.
>
> This kind of *forced repetition* (where you feel the pain of repeated work) can help you to figure
> out what (if any) shared logic you'd like to pull out.

Let's begin:

1. Start by filling in the `validation errors` nested `describe` block and the tests within it. I'm electing to copy two tests at once because these tests are very simple, and we already have a good idea of where we're going to end up with the implementation:

```
describe('addNew', () => {
  ...
    describe('validation errors', () => {
      describe('when the name is not provided', () => {
        let result;

        beforeEach(() => {
          result = addNew(
            createBirthday('', '1991-05-06')
          );
        });

        it('does not save the birthday', () => {
          expect(getAll()).toHaveLength(0);
        });

        it('returns an error', () => {
          expect(result).toEqual({
            error: 'Please provide a name.'
          });
        });
      });
    });
});
```

2. To make that pass in `src/lib/server/birthdayRepository.js`, start by defining the `empty` function at the bottom of the file:

```
const empty = (value) =>
  value === undefined ||
  value === null ||
  value.trim() === '';
```

3. Then, update the `addNew` method to include a guard class that uses the `empty` function. After this change, both tests should pass:

```
export const addNew = (item) => {
  if (empty(item.name)) {
```

```
        return { error: 'Please provide a name.' };
      }

      ...
    };
```

4. Now, we'll move on to the next nested `describe` block, for checking the date of birth format:

```
describe('when the date of birth is in the wrong format', () =>
{
  let result;

  beforeEach(() => {
    result = addNew(
      createBirthday('Hercules', 'unknown')
    );
  });

  it('does not save the birthday', () => {
    expect(getAll()).toHaveLength(0);
  });

  it('returns an error', () => {
    expect(result).toEqual({
      error:
        'Please provide a date of birth in the YYYY-
          MM-DD format.'
    });
  });
});
```

5. To make that pass, start by duplicating the `invalidDob` helper from the form action:

```
const invalidDob = (dob) => isNaN(Date.parse(dob));
```

6. Then, add the guard clause, which should cause both tests to pass:

```
if (invalidDob(item.dob)) {
  return {
    error:
      'Please provide a date of birth in the YYYY-MM-
        DD format.'
  };
}
```

7. Now, let's repeat the validation checks for the `replace` function. In the original form action tests, this wasn't necessary because we implemented the *edit form* functionality by building on the top of the original action for creating birthdays, so the validations were already there. But now, both operations are separated. Fill out the new nested `describe` block:

```
describe('replace', () => {
  ...
  describe('validation errors', () => {
    describe('when the name is not provided', () => {
      let result;

      beforeEach(() => {
        result = replace(
          storedId(),
          createBirthday('', '1991-05-06')
        );
      });

      it('does not update the birthday', () => {
        expect(getAll()[0].name).toEqual(
          'Hercules'
        );
      });

      it('returns an error', () => {
        expect(result).toEqual({
          error: 'Please provide a name.'
        });
      });
    });
  });
});
```

8. To make that pass, start by duplicating the same guard clause from `addNew`. We'll remove this duplication later:

```
export const replace = (id, item) => {
  if (empty(item.name)) {
    return { error: 'Please provide a name.' };
  }
  ...
};
```

9. Now, move on to the date of birth:

```
describe('when the date of birth is in the wrong format', () =>
{
  let result;

  beforeEach(() => {
    result = replace(
      storedId(),
      createBirthday('Hercules', 'unknown')
    );
  });

  it('does not update the birthday', () => {
    expect(getAll()[0].dob).toEqual(
      '1991-05-06'
    );
  });

  it('returns an error', () => {
    expect(result).toEqual({
      error:
        'Please provide a date of birth in the YYYY-
          MM-DD format.'
    });
  });
});
```

10. Make that pass by adding in the second guard clause, by repeating *step 6* but, this time, adding code within the `replace` function:

```
if (invalidDob(item.dob)) {
  return {
    error:
      'Please provide a date of birth in the YYYY-MM-
        DD format.'
  };
}
```

11. Then onto the final test. This one doesn't need a `describe` block since it's only one test:

```
it('requires an id of a birthday that exists in the store', ()
=> {
  expect(
    replace(
      '234',
```

```
          createBirthday('Hercules', '2009-01-02')
      )
  ).toEqual({
      error: 'An unknown ID was provided.'
  });
});
```

12. This time, put the guard clause right at the top. It seems to make sense that this guard should take precedence over the name and date of birth checks – notice, for example, how the argument comes first in the argument list:

```
export const replace = (id, item) => {
  if (!has(id))
    return { error: 'An unknown ID was provided.' };
  ...
}
```

That completes all the new functionality. All the `birthdayRepository` behavior is complete. Next, we'll stop to refactor to remove duplication.

Extracting common methods

In this section, we'll pull out the validation clauses that are duplicated in the `addNew` and `replace` functions, moving them into a shared `validate` function.

Let's start now with the `validate` function:

1. Below the definitions of `addNew` and `replace`, add the following function named `validate`. This contains the two guard clauses that appeared in each of the original functions. As a simplification, the `item` argument has been destructured into name and dob arguments:

```
const validate = ({ name, dob }) => {
  if (empty(name)) {
    return { error: 'Please provide a name.' };
  }

  if (invalidDob(dob)) {
    return {
      error:
        'Please provide a date of birth in the YYYY-
          MM-DD format.'
    };
  }
};
```

2. Then, update addNew to replace its guard clauses with a call to validate. The result is stored in validationResult, which can then be returned if it has a value:

```
export const addNew = (item) => {
  const validationResult = validate(item);
  if (validationResult) {
    return validationResult;
  }

  const id = randomUUID();
  const itemWithId = { ...item, id };
  db.set(id, itemWithId);
  return itemWithId;
};
```

3. Next, do the same for the replace function:

```
export const replace = (id, item) => {
  if (!has(id))
    return { error: 'An unknown ID was provided.' };

  const validationResult = validate(item);
  if (validationResult) {
    return validationResult;
  }

  const itemWithId = { ...item, id };
  db.set(id, itemWithId);
  return itemWithId;
};
```

4. Now, how about we pull out the last bit of each function? Add the set function:

```
const set = (id, item) => {
  const itemWithId = { ...item, id };
  db.set(id, itemWithId);
  return itemWithId;
};
```

5. Then, use that in addNew:

```
export const addNew = (item) => {
  const validationResult = validate(item);
  if (validationResult) {
    return validationResult;
  }
```

```
      return set(randomUUID(), item);
    };
```

6. And finally, add the same call at the end of the `replace` function:

```
    export const replace = (id, item) => {
      if (!has(id))
        return { error: 'An unknown ID was provided.' };

      const validationResult = validate(item);
      if (validationResult) {
        return validationResult;
      }

      return set(id, item);
    };
```

That completes the `birthdayRepository` implementation – a straightforward but satisfying refactoring.

Summary

This chapter has covered techniques for porting existing behavior from one place to another. In particular, it's shown how worthwhile it can be to move business logic out of framework objects – such as form actions – and into plain JavaScript objects. Doing so makes the tests simpler.

In this case, our tests were no longer asynchronous, and no longer needed to use the complex `performFormAction` helper.

Another benefit is that `birthdayRepository`, along with its validation, can be reused in other places. That's exactly what we'll do in the next chapter, when we introduce new API endpoints that interact with the repository.

10
Test-Driving API Endpoints

SvelteKit makes creating API endpoints a breeze. This chapter looks at how you can use tests to drive and prove your API endpoints.

In the preceding chapter, you saw how we could push business logic out of SvelteKit and into plain JavaScript. We can make use of the extracted `birthdayRepository` object in the new API endpoints. We will now add endpoints for creating, updating, and getting birthdays using the `addNew`, `replace`, and `getAll` functions from the repository.

Figure 10.1 shows how our system design is shaping up. The endpoints we'll create in this chapter are very lightweight, thanks to the fully specified `birthdayRepository` object:

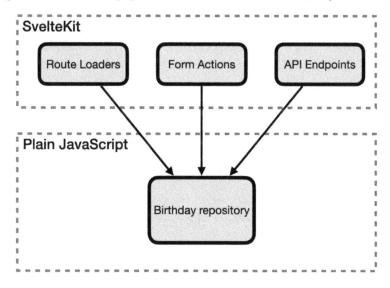

Figure 10.1 – SvelteKit components flowing into the inner system

We will cover the following key topics in this chapter:

- Creating a service test with Playwright

- Adding an API endpoint for retrieving data

- Adding an API endpoint for saving data

- Adding an API endpoint for updating data

By the end of the chapter, you'll have learned how to implement API endpoints using test-driven development.

Technical requirements

The code for the chapter can be found online at `https://github.com/PacktPublishing/Svelte-with-Test-Driven-Development/tree/main/Chapter10/Start`.

Creating a service test with Playwright

You've already seen how Playwright can be used to create end-to-end tests that drive the application through the web browser interface. It can also be used to drive the API endpoints directly, and that's what you'll learn to do in this section. The benefit of writing up-front Playwright API tests is that we can very carefully plan out how our API will look.

We'll write just a single test named `creating and reading a birthday`. It will do two things: first, create a request to `POST /api/birthdays` that will create a birthday. Then we'll call `GET /api/birthdays` and check that the previously created birthday is returned in the response:

1. Create a new file named `tests/api/birthdays.test.js` with the following content, which is the first half of that test:

```
import { expect, test } from '@playwright/test';

test('creating and reading a birthday', async ({
  request
}) => {
  const newBirthday = await request.post(
    '/api/birthdays',
    {
      data: {
        name: 'Nyx',
        dob: '1993-02-04'
      }
    }
  );
```

```
    expect(newBirthday.ok()).toBeTruthy();
});
```

The preceding code snippet uses the test's request parameter. It has a `request.post` method that we invoke to make the API request. The `data` prop is the JSON object we want to send across. Playwright takes care of converting that into an HTTP request and response. The request looks like this:

```
POST http://localhost:1234/api/birthdays
{
  "name": "Nyx",
  "dob": "1993-02-04"
}
```

The returned object, which we call `newBirthday`, has an `ok` method that we call to figure out whether the endpoint returned a `200` response.

Mixing assertions into test actions

In previous chapters, all our tests have been structured in the *Arrange-Act-Assert* format. When it comes to Playwright tests, it's okay to occasionally have repeated cycles of *Act-Assert*, ending up with something like *Arrange-Act-Assert-Act-Assert…*.

I wouldn't do that in my unit tests, but in end-to-end and service tests, it can sometimes make sense because they help the tests play out **user scenarios**. The tests follow the steps that a typical user would take. The assertions sprinkled throughout the test serve as checkpoints to check whether the test is on the right path.

---

2. Next, complete the test with a call to the GET `/api/birthdays` endpoint. Of interest here is the use of `expect.anything()` to say *I expect an ID back, but I don't care what it is*:

```
test('creating and reading a birthday', async ({
  request
}) => {
  ...

  const birthdays = await request.get(
    '/api/birthdays'
  );
  expect(birthdays.ok()).toBeTruthy();
  expect(await birthdays.json()).toEqual({
    birthdays: expect.arrayContaining([
      {
        name: 'Nyx',
        dob: '1993-02-04',
        id: expect.anything()
```

```
        }
      ])
    });
  });
```

That completes the test; go ahead and run the test and check that it currently fails (since the endpoint doesn't exist yet).

Avoiding data clashes in Playwright tests

The preceding example used the name `Nyx` in the test example. This name hasn't been used before, but if you had used one of the previous names, such as `Hercules` or `Athena`, you would have seen other tests fail.

The current Playwright test suite does not clear the test database between individual test runs. Here, we solved the issue by ensuring that each of our tests uses independent pieces of data.

An alternative approach would be to always clean down the database before each test or test suite, similar to how the Vitest unit tests are written.

There's an advantage to the first approach, however: you can point Playwright to deployed environments that are already primed with data that you don't control and still expect the tests to pass.

---

1. Add a second test for updating a birthday using the PUT HTTP verb. The request will look like this:

    ```
    PUT http://localhost:1234/api/birthday/abc123
    {
      "name": "Nyx",
      "dob": "1992-01-02"
    }
    ```

    Start with the first half of the test, given as follows. Notice how this pulls out the returned `id` field so that we can use it in the second half of the test:

    ```
    test('updating a birthday', async ({ request }) => {
      const newBirthday = await request.post(
        '/api/birthdays',
        {
          data: {
            name: 'Nyx',
            dob: '1993-02-04'
          }
        }
      );
      expect(newBirthday.ok()).toBeTruthy();
    ```

```
    const { id } = await newBirthday.json();
});
```

2. Then add the second half of the test, which performs the PUT request using id and checks the result:

```
test('updating a birthday', async ({ request }) => {
  ...

  const birthdays = await request.put(
    `/api/birthday/${id}`,
    {
      data: {
        name: 'Nyxx',
        dob: '1992-01-03'
      }
    }
  );
  expect(birthdays.ok()).toBeTruthy();

  const updatedBirthdays = await request.get(
    '/api/birthdays'
  );
  expect(await updatedBirthdays.json()).toEqual({
    birthdays: expect.arrayContaining([
      {
        name: 'Nyxx',
        dob: '1992-01-03',
        id
      }
    ])
  });
});
```

This last expectation doesn't make use of expect.anything. Instead, it checks that id remains the same.

That completes the two Playwright tests, covering the three new endpoints. In the next section, we'll use the GET request to retrieve all the birthdays from the system.

Adding an API endpoint for retrieving data

Now we get on to the fun bit: introducing new functionality for the API. In a SvelteKit application, a GET request is very directly specified by creating a function named GET inside of a route.

Although we won't use it for our endpoint, this function has a `params` argument that contains the `route` parameter. You'll see this later in the chapter when we implement the PUT request in the *Adding an API endpoint for updating data* section.

Valid responses from the endpoint must be proper response objects. We can use SvelteKit's JSON helper to define a valid JSON response. Error responses are handled by throwing an exception that is built by calling SvelteKit's error helper. We'll use both of these now.

> **The json helper in Node versions below 18**
>
> Calls to the `json` function may fail with a `Response is not defined` error. If you see this error when implementing the following tests, you can install the **node-fetch** package (`https://github.com/node-fetch/node-fetch`) and ensure it loads as part of your Vitest setup files.

Let's start by defining a new test suite:

1. Create a new test file, `src/routes/api/birthdays/server.test.js`, that begins with the following `import` statements. The `birthdayRepository` module is imported so that the repository can be populated before calling the GET function:

    ```
    import {
      describe, it, expect, beforeEach
    } from 'vitest';
    import {
      createBirthday
    } from 'src/factories/birthday.js';
    import
        as birthdayRepository
    from '$lib/server/birthdayRepository.js';
    import { GET } from './+server.js';
    ```

2. Next define the following helper method, `bodyOfResponse`, which we'll use in the first test to pull out data from the HTTP response. This can go just below the imports:

    ```
    const bodyOfResponse = (response) => response.json();
    ```

3. Then, create a new `describe` block with the following test. It creates two birthdays and checks that they are returned:

    ```
    describe('GET', () => {
      it('returns all the birthdays from the store', async
      () => {
        birthdayRepository.addNew(
          createBirthday('Hercules', '2010-04-05')
    ```

```
    );
  birthdayRepository.addNew(
    createBirthday('Ares', '2008-03-02')
  );
  const { birthdays } = await bodyOfResponse(GET());
  expect(birthdays).toEqual([
    expect.objectContaining(
      createBirthday('Hercules', '2010-04-05')
    ),
    expect.objectContaining(
      createBirthday('Ares', '2008-03-02')
    )
  ]);
  });
});
```

> **Testing array responses**
>
> I find that when I'm testing array objects, it's always best to use two (and sometimes three) items in the list rather than just one. That way, it's clear that the test is operating on lists of items, not just single items.

4. To make that test pass, create a new file named src/routes/api/birthdays/+server. js with the following content. The implementation works like this: it passes the request right through to the store using the getAll function and then wraps the response with a call to SvelteKit's json function:

```
import {
  getAll
} from '$lib/server/birthdayRepository.js';
import { json } from '@sveltejs/kit';

export const GET = () =>
  json({ birthdays: getAll() });
```

That completes the GET request. Next, we'll work on the POST and PUT requests.

Adding an API endpoint for saving data

In this section, we'll start by adding the POST request handler function for saving data and then continue with the PUT function, in its own route file, for updating data.

Let's begin with a test helper:

1. Create a new file, `src/factories/request.js`, with the following content. This will be used by both the POST and PUT functions to read the data of the request. SvelteKit will pass a Request argument. The only bit of this we need to provide is the `json` method, as shown here:

```
export const createRequest = (json) => ({
  json: () => Promise.resolve(json)
});
```

> **Providing minimal versions of collaborating objects**
>
> SvelteKit passes the Request objects into our request handler functions. But for our unit tests we don't need fully formed Request objects, we just need an object that implements the parts of the interface that we use. Our application code doesn't use anything but the json method for reading the request body in JSON format, so that's the only method we need.

2. Now move to `src/api/birthdays/server.test.js` and add an import statement for the createRequest method. Also, update the +server.js import to include the POST request handler function:

```
import {
  createRequest
} from 'src/factories/request.js';
import { GET, POST } from './+server.js';
```

3. Next, add a new describe block for the POST function, just below the describe block for the GET function, and include this one test:

```
describe('POST', () => {
  beforeEach(birthdayRepository.clear);

  it('saves the birthday in the store', async () => {
    await POST({
      request: createRequest(
        createBirthday('Hercules', '2009-03-01')
      )
    });
    expect(birthdayRepository.getAll()).toHaveLength(1
    );
    expect(birthdayRepository.getAll()[0]).toContain(
      createBirthday('Hercules', '2009-03-01')
    );
  });
});
```

4. To make that pass, first update the import in `src/api/birthdays/+server.js` to include the `addNew` function:

```
import {
  addNew,
  getAll
} from '$lib/server/birthdayRepository.js';
```

5. Continue by adding a definition for POST, as shown in the following code block. After this change, your test should pass:

```
export const POST = async ({ request }) => {
  const { name, dob } = await request.json();
  addNew({ name, dob });
};
```

6. Now that we have data saved into the repository, it's time to check the HTTP response. We want any API caller to receive the same data back. The following test makes use of the `toContain` matcher rather than `toEqual`. That's because we already know that the response will contain an `id` field that isn't relevant to this test:

```
it('returns a json response with the data', async () => {
  const response = await POST({
    request: createRequest(
      createBirthday('Hercules', '2009-03-01')
    )
  });
  expect(await bodyOfResponse(response)).toContain(
    createBirthday('Hercules', '2009-03-01')
  );
});
```

> **Testing the presence of an id field**
>
> Why is the `id` field not included in the expectation of this test? Because it has a different lifecycle from the other data. This test verifies that the user-provided information is stored. But the `id` field is auto-generated, so it belongs to a separate test. I've omitted it here because it's already tested in both the repository and the Playwright API test, but you may feel more comfortable including the test.

7. To make the test pass, add a `return` value to the function that uses the `json` function import:

```
export const POST = async ({ request }) => {
  const { name, dob } = await request.json();
  const result = addNew({ name, dob });
```

```
    return json(result);
  };
```

8. The final test for the POST request handler is to check that the function throws an exception if the data is invalid. Throwing errors can complicate tests: here, the test uses a call to expect. hasAssertions to ensure that Vitest will fail the test if the call does *not* raise an error:

```
it('throws an error if the data is invalid', async () => {
  expect.hasAssertions();
  try {
    await POST({
      request: createRequest(
        createBirthday('Ares', '')
      )
    });
  } catch (error) {
    expect(error.status).toEqual(422);
    expect(error.body).toEqual({
      message:
        'Please provide a date of birth in the YYYY-
          MM-DD format.'
    });
  }
});
```

Try running this test now: you'll see the expected any number of assertions, but got none failure. That is courtesy of the hasAssertions statement at the top of the test.

> **Understanding the hasAssertions helper**
>
> Try deleting the expect.hasAssertions line from the test. You will notice that the test already passes. That's because the expectations were never met. This is the point of the hasAssertions call: it is useful in tests that rely on having expectations within catch blocks that won't be called until you implement the exception-throwing behavior in your application code.

9. To make that pass, first update the import statement in src/api/birthdays/+server. js to include the error helper:

```
import { json, error } from '@sveltejs/kit';
```

10. Then update the POST function to re-package any errors from the repository into an error object that's then thrown:

```
export const POST = async ({ request }) => {
  const { name, dob } = await request.json();
  const result = addNew({ name, dob });
  if (result.error) throw error(422, result.error);
  return json(result);
};
```

That completes the POST request handler for inserting new birthdays; the next section completes the chapter with the addition of the PUT request handler for updating existing birthdays.

Adding an API endpoint for updating data

The final piece of the puzzle is to add a PUT request handler function for dealing with updates. Similar to the POST function, we must provide the request body using the createRequest helper.

The form of our PUT request means that id is passed as a parameter in the URL, like this:

Here's a reminder of how the URL must be passed:

```
PUT http://localhost:1234/api/birthday/abc123
```

To make SvelteKit register the abc123 value as a parameter, we need to create a new route directory at src/routes/api/birthday/[id]. SvelteKit will then know that abc123 matches the [id] bit of the directory path. The directory itself will then contain the +server.js file and its tests.

Let's start with the tests:

1. Create a new file named src/routes/api/birthday/[id]/server.test.js and add the following imports. This has everything we've used previously for the GET and POST functions, together with an import for the PUT function:

```
import {
  describe,
  it,
  expect,
  beforeEach
} from 'vitest';
import
    as birthdayRepository
from '$lib/server/birthdayRepository.js';
import {
  createBirthday
} from 'src/factories/birthday.js';
```

```
import {
  createRequest
} from 'src/factories/request.js';
import { PUT } from './+server.js';
```

2. Then create this new `describe` block. It contains a `beforeEach` block that not only clears the repository but inserts a new item, ready for editing:

```
describe('PUT', () => {
  beforeEach(() => {
    birthdayRepository.clear();
    birthdayRepository.addNew(
      createBirthday('Hercules', '2009-03-01')
    );
  });
});
```

3. Before we get to the first test, add the following helper:

```
const storedId = () =>
  birthdayRepository.getAll()[0].id;
```

4. Now add the first test, as shown here. It mimics SvelteKit's call semantics by passing a new `params` object into the handler:

```
it('updates the birthday in the store', async () => {
  await PUT({
    request: createRequest(
      createBirthday('Hercules', '1999-03-01')
    ),
    params: { id: storedId() }
  });
  expect(birthdayRepository.getAll()).toHaveLength(1);
  expect(birthdayRepository.getAll()[0]).toContain(
    createBirthday('Hercules', '1999-03-01')
  );
});
```

5. To make that pass, create a new file named `src/routes/api/birthday/[id]/+server.js` with the following content. This should immediately make the test pass:

```
import {
  replace
} from '$lib/server/birthdayRepository.js';

export const PUT = async ({
```

```
    request,
    params: { id }
  }) => {
    const { name, dob } = await request.json();
    const result = replace(id, { name, dob });
  };
```

6. For the next test, we'll begin by repeating a helper from the GET tests. Add the bodyOfResponse function, as shown here:

```
const bodyOfResponse = (response) => response.json();
```

7. Then, add the next test, which uses this function to check the response:

```
it('returns a json response with the data', async () => {
  const response = await PUT({
    request: createRequest(
      createBirthday('Hercules', '1999-03-01')
    ),
    params: { id: storedId() }
  });
  expect(await bodyOfResponse(response)).toContain(
    createBirthday('Hercules', '1999-03-01', {
      id: storedId()
    })
  );
});
```

8. To make that pass, start by adding the import for json in the application code:

```
import { json } from '@sveltejs/kit';
```

9. Then, update the PUT function to return the result of the repository action, just as we did with the POST request handler function:

```
export const PUT = async ({
  request,
  params: { id }
}) => {
  const { name, dob } = await request.json();
  const result = replace(id, { name, dob });

  return json(result);
};
```

10. The final test repeats the mechanics of the final POST test, checking what happens if the data is invalid:

```
it('throws an error if the data is invalid', async () => {
  expect.hasAssertions();
  try {
    await PUT({
      request: createRequest(
        createBirthday('Hercules', '')
      ),
      params: { id: storedId() }
    });
  } catch (error) {
    expect(error.status).toEqual(422);
    expect(error.body).toEqual({
      message:
        'Please provide a date of birth in the YYYY-
          MM-DD format.'
    });
  }
});
```

11. To make that pass, start by updating the import statement in the application code to include the error function:

```
import { json, error } from '@sveltejs/kit';
```

12. Finally, include the guard clause in the PUT function, as shown here:

```
export const PUT = async ({
  request,
  params: { id }
}) => {
  const { name, dob } = await request.json();
  const result = replace(id, { name, dob });
  if (result.error) throw error(422, result.error);

  return json(result);
};
```

That's it. If you run both the Vitest and Playwright tests now, you should find they all pass.

Summary

This chapter has shown how to make quick work of API endpoints. Playwright tests can be used to specify how an API should behave, and the unit tests can be used to drive the design and ensure that we end up with minimal implementation.

The next chapter completes the API story arc: we will update the form actions to use the new API endpoints rather than going directly to the repository.

11

Replacing Behavior with a Side-By-Side Implementation

In the previous two chapters you built out a fully formed repository and an API for accessing it. Now it's time to complete the story arc by updating both the SvelteKit loader and form actions to use the API instead of the repository.

It's worth pointing out that this isn't a necessary step: it would be perfectly acceptable to keep the SvelteKit server pieces pointing directly at the repository.

But reworking our existing code to point at the new API endpoints will introduce you to two ideas: first, that of a **side-by-side implementation**, which is a way to use tests to replace the existing code while ensuring the test suite remains on *Green*. The second is the use of a test double to shield the unit tests from SvelteKit. The test double takes the place of the framework code, avoiding a real network call out to the API – which wouldn't work anyway since the API isn't running within our Vitest test suite.

Figure 11.1 shows two views of our code base. The left side shows how the new architecture of our application code will look, with the SvelteKit route loaders and form actions pointing to the API endpoints. The right side shows how the unit tests for the router loaders and form actions will see the world. In this setup, the API endpoints are not accessed at all.

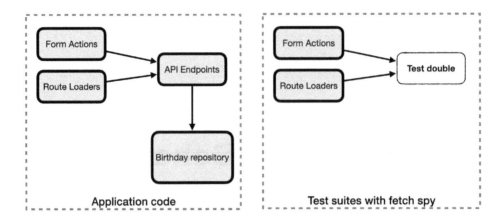

Figure 11.1 – Using a test double to plug SvelteKit behavior within unit test suites

After updating our SvelteKit components, we'll wrap things up by updating the Playwright test to use the new API and stop the database seed data from appearing in test environments (both Playwright and Vitest).

This chapter covers the following key topics:

- Updating the route loader to use the API
- Updating the page form action to use the API
- Using a server hook to seed sample data

By the end of the chapter, you'll have seen how to use a **spy** (a form of test double) and the process of building a side-by-side implementation.

Technical requirements

The code for the chapter can be found online at `https://github.com/PacktPublishing/Svelte-with-Test-Driven-Development/tree/main/Chapter11/Start`.

Updating the route loader to use the API

In this section, you'll introduce a call to the `GET /api/birthdays` endpoint using the SvelteKit fetch function. That will involve using a spy.

> **What is a test spy?**
>
> A spy is a function that keeps a record of each time it is called, together with the arguments it is called with. It can then be inspected later to verify that it was called with the correct arguments. The spy is almost always a *stub* as well, meaning it avoids calling the real function entirely, instead returning a hardcoded – stubbed – value. The spy acts as a substitute for a real function.
>
> In Vitest, a spy is created by calling the `vi.fn` function.

When we use a test spy, you'll have at least one test that checks the arguments passed to the spy. Then you'll have at least one more test for each stubbed return value that the spy returns.

We will use a spy for the `fetch` function that mimics retrieving birthdays via the GET `/api/birthdays` endpoint.

> **Understanding the SvelteKit fetch function**
>
> SvelteKit provides a `fetch` parameter to the user-defined `load` function and to the form actions. The value of this parameter is a function that has the same semantics as the standard Fetch API provided by browsers. The difference is in mechanics: SvelteKit's `fetch` function is able to short-cut calls made on the server so that they don't cause an HTTP request but instead feed directly into the GET function that matches the route specified.

Let's begin with a new factory method definition:

1. Create a new file named `src/factories/fetch.js` and add the following definition. We will use this to build stub `Response` objects that the test spy will return:

   ```
   export const fetchResponseOk = (response = {}) => ({
     status: 'ok',
     json: () => Promise.resolve(response)
   });
   ```

2. Now open the test file at `src/routes/birthdays/page.server.test.js` and add an `import` statement to that function:

   ```
   import {
     fetchResponseOk
   } from 'src/factories/fetch.js';
   ```

3. Next, update the Vitest `import` statement to include an import for `vi`, like this:

   ```
   import {
     describe,
     it,
     expect,
   ```

```
    beforeEach,
    vi
} from 'vitest';
```

4. Add the following test at the bottom of the describe block with the title /birthdays - load. In addition to creating a test spy with a call to vi.fn(), this also uses the mockResolvedValue function to specify that the spy should return a value wrapped in a Promise object. The test concludes with the toBeCalledWith matcher to verify that the spy is called in the right way:

```
describe('/birthdays - load', () => {
    ...


    it('calls fetch with /api/birthdays', async () => {
        const fetch = vi.fn();
        fetch.mockResolvedValue(fetchResponseOk());
        const result = await load({ fetch });
        expect(fetch).toBeCalledWith('/api/birthdays');
    });
});
```

5. To make that pass, we'll start with a side-by-side implementation. That means the previous implementation remains in place alongside the new implementation. In the src/routes/birthdays/+page.server.js file, modify the load function so that it takes a fetch argument and then invokes it as the first thing it does, like this:

```
export const load = ({ fetch }) => {
    fetch('/api/birthdays');
    return {
        birthdays: getAll()
    }
};
```

This will cause the original test case to fail due to a missing value for fetch. We are about to delete this test, but for now, let's humor ourselves by fixing the test.

6. Update the test case to use a very simple stub value for fetch, as shown in the following code. This highlights the fact that a Vitest spy created by vi.fn is not always necessary. If you're not checking the spy, then a plain stub is enough:

```
describe('/birthdays - load', () => {
    it('returns a fixture of two items', () => {
        const result = load({ fetch: () => {} });
        ...
    });
});
```

7. Continue by writing the second test, which checks that the `load` function returns whatever data came back from `fetch`. This time, we need to pass an actual value to `fetchResponseOk`, and compare that to the `return` value:

```
describe('/birthdays - load', () => {
  ...
  it('returns the response body', async () => {
    const birthdays = [
      createBirthday('Hercules', '1994-02-02'),
      createBirthday('Athena', '1989-01-01')
    ];
    const fetch = vi.fn();
    fetch.mockResolvedValue(
      fetchResponseOk({ birthdays })
    );
    const result = await load({ fetch });
    expect(result).toEqual({ birthdays });
  });
});
```

8. Go ahead and update the `load` function to return this value:

```
export const load = async ({ fetch }) => {
  const result = await fetch('/api/birthdays');
  return result.json();
};
```

9. You might have noticed this is in direct conflict with the original test we wrote. When we build a side-by-side implementation, the final step is often switching out the return value. When that happens, it's time to delete the original test. So, go ahead and delete the original test – the only one titled *returns a fixture of two items* – since it no longer applies.

10. Finally, remove the `getAll` import from the `+page.server.js` file:

```
import {
  addNew,
  replace
} from '$lib/server/birthdayRepository.js';
```

You've now seen how to use `vi.fn` to create a test spy for testing `fetch` calls and a basic side-by-side implementation. The next section repeats the same process for the page form action, but this time the implementation is more complex.

Updating the page form action to use the API

In the section, we will update the page form action to use the new POST and PUT methods on the API endpoints instead of the addNew and replace functions of the repository.

This will be done using the same side-by-side technique of the previous section, but this time it's more involved. We still need tests to verify that the spy is called with the right parameters and that the return value is given. But now we also need to verify that errors are converted to SvelteKit form failures, since the form action has separate handling for errors.

Another important change here is that we will use two tests for checking the parameters passed to the fetch call. This is a powerful technique when faced with complex arguments where there are *clumps* of arguments that have separate meanings.

In the case of fetch, the URL and the HTTP verb are one *clump*: we can have a single test that verifies, for example, that we're calling the POST /api/birthdays endpoint. But there's also the body property, and since that isn't static data – it changes depending on the form action input parameters – it seems sensible to give that a test of its own.

Finally, since the API endpoints are performing data validation, we no longer need that functionality. So we'll finish by deleting that implementation and its related tests.

Let's get started by updating the existing describe block with some new setup:

1. Find the describe block named /birthdays - default action and add the following three pieces of setup: a fetch variable that can be accessed in all tests; a new beforeEach block to set up the fetch response; and an updated performFormAction method that passes in the fetch argument:

    ```
    describe('/birthdays - default action', () => {
      const fetch = vi.fn();

      beforeEach(() => {
        fetch.mockResolvedValue(fetchResponseOk());
      });

      const performFormAction = (formData) =>
        actions.default({
          request: createFormDataRequest(formData),
          fetch
        });
      ...
    });
    ```

2. Then, add this new nested `describe` block with its single test below all the existing tests. It checks that the `fetch` spy has been called with the correct URL and `method` of POST:

```
describe('when adding a new birthday', () => {
  it('requests data from POST /api/birthdays', async
  () => {
    await performFormAction(
      createBirthday('Zeus', '2009-02-02')
    );
    expect(fetch).toBeCalledWith(
      '/api/birthdays',
      expect.objectContaining({ method: 'POST' })
    );
  });
});
```

3. To make that pass, start by adding the `fetch` argument into the form action:

```
export const actions = {
  default: async ({ request, fetch }) => {
    ...
  }
}
```

4. Then, make a start on the side-by-side implementation. Find the call to `addNew`, and just below it, add a new call to `fetch`, as shown here:

```
let result;
if (id) {
  ...
} else {
  result = addNew({ name, dob });
  await fetch('/api/birthdays', {
    method: 'POST'
  });
}
```

5. For the next test, we have a very similar test which is still testing the arguments to the `fetch` spy, but this time checking the varying portion of it: the `body` property. Add that test now:

```
it('sends the birthday as the request body', async () => {
  await performFormAction(
    createBirthday('Zeus', '2009-02-02')
  );
  expect(fetch).toBeCalledWith(
    expect.anything(),
    expect.objectContaining({
```

```
        body: JSON.stringify({
          name: 'Zeus',
          dob: '2009-02-02'
        })
      })
    );
  });
```

The preceding code sample makes use of a helper function called expect.anything, which you also saw in *Chapter 10, Test-Driving API Endpoints*. Since we already have a previous test that checks the value of the first argument, we can avoid repeating ourselves by checking it here and simultaneously relax the expectation so that the tests are kept independent of each other.

Using this helper also aids with the readability of the test by focusing the reader's attention on what's specifically of interest: the second argument, not the first.

6. To make that pass, update the fetch call from *step 4* to include the body property:

```
await fetch('/api/birthdays', {
  method: 'POST',
  body: JSON.stringify({ name, dob })
});
```

7. Now let's handle the error case. For this, we need a new factory for an error response. In src/factories/fetch.js, add the following definition for fetchResponseError:

```
export const fetchResponseError = (errorMessage) => ({
  status: 'error',
  json: () =>
    Promise.resolve({ message: errorMessage })
});
```

8. Then import it into your test suite:

```
import {
  fetchResponseOk,
  fetchResponseError
} from 'src/factories/fetch.js';
```

9. We're ready for the next test. This test checks what happens when an error occurs. Since our spy has no real logic, we don't care about the *specifics* of the error. We just need it to trigger the same behavior as the real code. That means having a non-ok status message, just like the fetchResponseError factory gives us. To make it clear that it's not real logic, I've used an error message string as opposed to a real error message:

```
it('returns a 422 if the POST request returns an error', async
() => {
```

```
fetch.mockResolvedValue(
  fetchResponseError('error message')
);
const result = await performFormAction(
  createBirthday('Zeus', '2009-02-02')
);

expect(result).toBeUnprocessableEntity({
  error: 'error message',
  name: 'Zeus',
  dob: '2009-02-02'
});
});
```

10. To make this pass, start by saving the response from the `fetch` call in the form action:

```
let result;
let response;
if (id) {
  ...
} else {
  result = addNew({ name, dob });
  response = await fetch('/api/birthdays', {
    method: 'POST',
    body: JSON.stringify({ name, dob })
  });
}
```

11. Then, add the following return clause *after* the existing error clause for the original `result` value. This is a trick of the side-by-side implementation. It ensures that the original implementation won't fail on us:

```
if (!response.ok) {
  const { message } = await response.json();
  return fail(422, {
    id,
    name,
    dob,
    error: message
  });
}
```

12. All right, let's do the same for the `replace` call. Add the following new nested `describe` block with a single test:

```
describe('when replacing an existing birthday', () => {
  it('requests data from PUT /api/birthday/{id}',
  async () => {
    await performFormAction(
      createBirthday('Zeus', '2009-02-02', {
        id: '123'
      })
    );
    expect(fetch).toBeCalledWith(
      '/api/birthday/123',
      expect.objectContaining({ method: 'PUT' })
    );
  });
});
```

13. In the application code, find the call to `replace`, and just below it, add a new call to `fetch`. After this, the test should pass:

```
if (id) {
  result = replace(id, { name, dob });
  await fetch(`/api/birthday/${id}`, {
    method: 'PUT'
  });
} else {
  ...
}
```

14. Next, we'll test the body of the PUT request. Because we're not actually calling into the repository, it no longer matters whether the item exists or not. It's all down to the test double setup:

```
it('sends the birthday as the request body', async () => {
  await performFormAction(
    createBirthday('Zeus', '2009-02-02', {
      id: '123'
    })
  );
  expect(fetch).toBeCalledWith(
    expect.anything(),
    expect.objectContaining({
      body: JSON.stringify({
        name: 'Zeus',
        dob: '2009-02-02'
```

```
        })
      })
    );
  });
```

15. To make that pass, add the `body` property to the `fetch` call:

```
await fetch(`/api/birthday/${id}`, {
  method: 'PUT',
  body: JSON.stringify({ name, dob })
});
```

16. For the final test, repeat the same process used for the `POST` request. We use `mockResolvedValue` combined with the `fetchResponseError` factory to make the spy trigger our error flow:

```
it('returns a 422 if the POST request returns an error', async
() => {
  fetch.mockResolvedValue(
    fetchResponseError('error message')
  );
  const result = await performFormAction(
    createBirthday('Zeus', '2009-02-02', {
      id: '123'
    })
  );

  expect(result).toBeUnprocessableEntity({
    error: 'error message',
    name: 'Zeus',
    dob: '2009-02-02',
    id: '123'
  });
});
```

17. To make that pass, simply save the result in the `response` variable. The code will then rely on the same return clause from *step 11*:

```
if (id) {
  result = replace(id, { name, dob });
  response = await fetch('/api/birthdays', {
    method: 'POST',
    body: JSON.stringify({ name, dob })
  });
} ...
```

18. Now comes the satisfying bit. You can go ahead and delete the original implementation, first by deleting the tests, then by deleting the code itself. Delete all these tests:

- `adds a new birthday into the list`

- `saves unique ids onto each new birthday`

- `updates an entry that shares the same id`

- `when the name is not provided...`

- `when the date of birth in the wrong format...`

- `when the id is unknown...`

- `returns the id when an empty name is provided`

- `returns the id when an empty date of birth is provided`

> **Using the online code repository**
> This is a lot of code change. You can use the online repository to cross-check your changes as you go along.

19. You can delete the import for `birthayRepository`, since you're no longer using that, and the `storedId` method too. If you run your tests now, you should find they still pass.

20. Go ahead and delete all the bits from the implementation that reference the birthday repository:

- The calls to `addNew` and `replace`

- The `result` variable and the error handling

- The `import` statement for the `replace` function (although the `addNew` function is still needed; we'll remove it in the next section)

That completes the new version of the page form actions. But before finishing, we need to do something about our seed data.

Using a server hook to seed sample data

In the early chapters of the book, we added seed data into the `/birthdays` route in the `src/routes/birthdays/+page.server.js` file. At the top, there are two calls to `addNew` to create two fake birthdays. We relied on this data within our Playwright tests. It's now time to clean up.

> **Creating repeated data in the development environment**
>
> If you've been running the dev server while you edited files, you will have noticed that as SvelteKit reloaded your files, the fake birthdays were repeatedly created, resulting in many birthday objects in the system. This was because of those `addNew` calls at the top of the route's `+page.server.js` file. Another problem caused by our seed data will now be fixed.

First, we'll update the Playwright tests to create all their test data via the API. Then we'll remove the hardcoded seed data from our system. Finally, we will bring the seed data back when loading the development environment.

That means the seed data is available using the `npm run dev` command but won't be there when running the automated tests or when launching in production mode.

Let's start with the Playwright tests:

1. Add the following to the top of `tests/birthdays.test.js`, which is a new function to make a `POST /api/birthdays` request to insert a birthday into the repository:

    ```
    const addBirthday = async (request, { name, dob }) => {
      await request.post('/api/birthdays', {
        data: { name, dob }
      });
    };
    ```

2. Then, update the `list all birthdays` test so that it begins with two calls to `addBirthday`, like this:

    ```
    test('lists all birthday', async ({ page, request }) => {
      await addBirthday(request, {
        name: 'Hercules',
        dob: '1995-02-03'
      });
      await addBirthday(request, {
        name: 'Athena',
        dob: '1995-02-03'
      });
      ...
    });
    ```

3. Next, update the `edits a birthday` test in the same way:

    ```
    test('edits a birthday', async ({ page, request }) => {
      await addBirthday(request, {
        name: 'Ares',
        dob: '1985-01-01'
    ```

```
    });
    ...
  });
```

4. Before running the Playwright tests, we need to remove the seed data. In `src/routes/birthdays/+page.server.js`, delete the two calls to `addNew` and the `addNew` import statement.

5. Run the Playwright tests and verify they've passed.

6. All that's left is to add a server hook for that data so that when you run the server in dev mode, you get some data. Create a new file named `src/hooks.server.js` with the following content. SvelteKit will automatically load this file when the web server is launched:

```
import {
  addNew
} from '$lib/server/birthdayRepository.js';

if (import.meta.env.MODE === 'development') {
  addNew({ name: 'Hercules', dob: '1994-02-02' });
  addNew({ name: 'Athena', dob: '1989-01-01' });
}
```

That completes the removal of the hardcoded seed data.

Summary

This chapter introduced you to the concept of a test double that can be used to block out unwanted framework behavior. In our case, that was the `fetch` call that, at runtime, will be magically hooked up to the API endpoints. But since we don't have access to the SvelteKit runtime environment within a Vitest unit test, we stubbed it out.

You also learned how a side-by-side implementation is used to keep your test suites on *Green* while you systematically replace the internals of a function.

The next chapter continues the theme of test doubles with a detailed look at component mocks.

12

Using Component Mocks to Clarify Tests

The preceding chapter introduced the concept of a test double and showed how `vi.fn` can be used to swap out unwanted behavior within your Vitest test suites. The same technique can be used for Svelte components, but it's a little more complicated.

Imagine you're writing unit tests for a component named `Parent`, and that component itself renders another developer-defined component, named `Child`. By default, when your tests render `Parent`, `Child` is rendered too. But using a component mock can stop that from happening. It swaps out the real `Child` for a test double.

There are various reasons why you'd want to do this:

- The `Child` component already has its own unit test suite, and you don't want to repeat yourself (a form of overtesting, described in detail in the *Avoiding component mocks* section)

- The `Child` component has behavior on mount, such as fetching data via the Fetch API, that you'd rather avoid running within your test

- The `Child` component comes from a third-party library and it's more important that you verify the props it is rendered with, rather than verifying the behavior of the third-party component itself

The downside of using component mocks is that they're complex, and if you're not careful, they can become a burden.

> **Staying safe with test doubles**
>
> The number-one rule when using component mocks, and test doubles in general, is to avoid building any control logic (`if` statements and loops) into them. Instead, when you use `mockReturnValue` or `mockResolvedValue` to specify the value that is returned, always prefer to return fixed values.
>
> An easy way to ensure that happens is to ensure that each unit test gets its own test double instance. In other words, avoid setting up a test double in a `beforeEach` block and reusing it across all tests.
>
> If you're struggling to keep test doubles simple, that can be a sign that the application code design is too complex. Try reconfiguring the object under test, perhaps by splitting it out into a number of separate objects.

This chapter covers the following topics:

- Avoiding component mocks when possible
- Using hand-rolled component stubs
- Using a component mock library

By the end of the chapter, you will be confident with using component mocking techniques and know when to use them.

Technical requirements

The code for the chapter can be found online at `https://github.com/PacktPublishing/Svelte-with-Test-Driven-Development/tree/main/Chapter12/Start`.

Avoiding component mocks

This section covers how to build your application without using component mocks. Of course, the application we've built up to this point hasn't used any, so you already know it's possible.

The SvelteKit application we've built has a page route component that renders a list of `Birthday` components and a `BirthdayForm` component. Both of these components are covered by their own test suites, so they are certainly candidates for using component mocks. The page route component would simply check that it renders `Birthday` and `BirthdayForm` in the right way, and avoid testing any of the birthdays themselves.

But there's not much point in doing this. Neither of these components has any behavior on mount, so there's no trouble in letting them render.

The biggest risk you have in not using component mocks is that of **overtesting**. This is when you repeat the tests of a child component in the tests for the parent component. In our example application, it would be like taking all the tests in the `Birthday` component test suite and repeating them in the page route test suite.

Figure 12.1 shows how the test suites for a `Parent` and `Child` component can be developed without overtesting. The `Parent` test suite only needs to test a single flow to `Child` to prove the connection. If there are any interesting return flows of data back from `Child` into `Parent` (such as component event bindings), then they should be tested too.

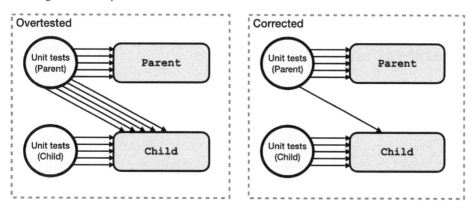

Figure 12.1 – Overtesting caused by repeated tests at two levels in a component hierarchy

Thankfully, TDD has a couple of rules that avoid the problem of overtesting.

Avoiding overtesting using TDD

Imagine first that you're building your application using a bottom-up approach, which is the approach this book has followed. That means that you write the `Child` component and its test suite before writing the `Parent` component and its test suite.

When you begin test-driving `Parent`, you write a test that will bring in the `Child` component. (The test description might be something such as *displays the birthday information*.) Recall the TDD rule of *make the simplest change that could possibly work*. Since you've already written the `Child` component at your disposal, then the simplest change is to simply bring in the `Child` component.

Then, the rule of the *Red* test comes into play, and this is the crucial one that avoids overtesting. You can't work on a test unless you see it fail. But if your first test brought in the `Child` component, you suddenly get all the behavior of `Child` for free. So, if you're following TDD, it's impossible to write a *Red* test for all the behavior of `Child`, because it will already pass.

Now imagine that you started by building the `Parent` component and at some point felt the urge to extract a `Child` component (you might think of this as a top-down approach). How do you go about extracting `Child`? If you're being strict, you might start by rewriting the tests for `Child`, as we did in *Chapter 9, Extracting Logic Out of the Framework*, when we extracted the birthday repository. But generally, you wouldn't stop there: you'd want to go back and delete those extra tests from `Parent`.

You could view this as part of the *Refactor* step of the TDD cycle. In fact, we did this in the preceding chapter when we ended up deleting a bunch of tests as we changed out the system functionality.

To repeat the message of this section: you don't always need to use mocks. If you have a single test to prove the connection between `Parent` and `Child`, that's often enough. Moreover, using TDD can naturally lead to you using this approach.

Using hand-rolled component stubs

In this section, we'll look at a simple but effective way of mocking components, by building hand-rolled component stubs. This isn't as clever as using a component mock library, but it's simpler and easier to understand. Often, the simplest approach is the best choice.

To recap what we're trying to do: we have a child component that we want to avoid rendering, perhaps because it has mount behavior or it's a complex third-party component.

Hand-rolled component stubs rely on Vitest's `vi.mock` function combined with a special __mocks__ directory. You create a stub component with the same name as your component, but inside a __mocks__ directory at the same level as the component itself. Then, you instruct Vitest to use the mock using the `vi.mock` statement placed at the top of your test file. This will mean the entire test suite uses the mock.

We can demonstrate this using the page route component test suite, building mocks for the `Birthday` and `BirthdayForm` components. These components don't have any side effects on mount, and they aren't third party, but they do have their own test suites. So, even though it doesn't feel necessary to make this change, it's not unsafe to do so.

Since this work isn't necessary, we'll build an example test suite in a test file named `page.mocks.test.js`. Although this isn't how I'd do this in the real world, it does highlight how you can have both mocked and non-mocked unit tests within the same code base.

We'll start with a look at how to verify props using a stub component. Then, we'll look at checking the ordering of instances, followed by dealing with complex prop verification, and finishing with a look at how to dispatch component events.

Rendering all props within a component stub

In the preceding chapter, you saw that it's important to verify the props that are passed into a test double. Component stubs are no different. The way we do this is to ensure that the component stub renders all the props and then use standard DOM matchers to verify their presence.

Let's begin by creating a hand-rolled component stub for the `Birthday` component:

1. Create a new directory named `src/routes/birthdays/__mocks__`. The special name is picked up automatically by Vitest as a location for your mocks.

2. Create a new file named `src/routes/birthdays/__mocks__/Birthday.svelte` with the following content. It does nothing but render out all the props that are passed in:

```svelte
<script>
  export let name;
  export let dob;
</script>

<div>
  {name}
  {dob}
</div>
```

3. Now create a new test file named `src/routes/birthdays/page.mock.test.js` and start with the usual `import` statements. Notice how `vi` is included; we'll use that in the next step:

```js
import {
  describe,
  it,
  expect,
  vi
} from 'vitest';
import {
  render,
  screen
} from '@testing-library/svelte';
import { click } from '@testing-library/user-event';
import {
  createBirthday
} from 'src/factories/birthday.js';
import Page from './+page.svelte';
```

4. Next, just below the `import` statements, add a call to `vi.mock`. The path given must match the path to the *actual* `Birthday` component. Vitest will pick up the mock and load that instead:

```js
vi.mock('./Birthday.svelte');
```

5. Now, start a new `describe` block, together with a sample `birthdays` array. All our tests will use this:

```js
describe('/birthdays', () => {
  const birthdays = [
    createBirthday('Hercules', '1994-02-02', {
      id: '123'
    }),
```

```
      createBirthday('Athena', '1989-01-01', {
        id: '234'
      })
   ];
});
```

6. Time for the first test. This is going to check that given the two birthdays defined previously, each of the correct bits of information is displayed on screen:

```
it('displays a Birthday component for each birthday', () => {
  render(Page, { data: { birthdays } });
  expect(
    screen.queryByText(/Hercules/)
  ).toBeVisible();
  expect(
    screen.queryByText(/1994-02-02/)
  ).toBeVisible();
  expect(
    screen.queryByText(/Athena/)
  ).toBeVisible();
  expect(
    screen.queryByText(/1989-01-01/)
  ).toBeVisible();
});
```

Testing lists of components

This test checks *two* birthdays, not one: since we're interested in the listing behavior – one `Birthday` component per entry – it's important to test that a list of birthdays does in fact give a list of `Birthday` components. A single birthday isn't enough to prove a list.

---

7. Because our implementation already exists, this test should already pass. But it's important to prove the test works, and this time we want to also verify that the mock has been picked up. So, first delete the contents of the *actual* `Birthday` component (not the mock). The test should *still* pass. (Make sure you use the `v src/routes/birthdays/page.mocks.test.js` command to run your tests, otherwise you'll see all the failures from other test suites.) This should convince you that the mock is being picked up.

8. Undo your changes to the `Birthday` component, and now let's make a change to make the test fail. In the page route component at `src/routes/birthday/+page.svelte`, comment out the rendering of the `Birthday` component, like this:

```
<!--Birthday
  name={birthday.name}
  dob={birthday.dob}
/-->
```

9. Run the tests with `v src/routes/birthdays/page.mocks.test.js` and verify the test now fails. Then, undo your change.

You've now learned about the basic usage of component stubs.

Checking the ordering of component instances

Sometimes, when we are dealing with lists of components, we want to check the ordering of instances. We can check that using the `data-testid` attribute to get hold of each specific instance.

There is a general piece of advice to avoid using `data-testid` in tests. This is good advice, but your component stubs are a part of your test suite, not the application code, so it's safe to use them here.

> **When to use list ordering tests**
>
> The test in this section isn't very TDD-like; it proves what I'd consider the *default* ordering of lists. If you already have a test that checks that data is listed, like the one in *step 6* of the preceding section, then the simplest way to make that pass is to implement the default ordering. So, writing a test like the one in *writing a test like the one your'e about to see* will likely pass by default, and is therefore an invalid test.

Let's start:

1. Update the component stub to add a `data-testid` attribute, like this:

```
<script>
  export let name;
  export let dob;
</script>

<div data-testid="Birthday">
  {name}
  {dob}
</div>
```

2. Now, write a test that proves the ordering. It uses `queryAllByTestId` to return a list of elements that match a specific `data-testid` attribute value, in the order they are listed in the document:

```
it('displays the Birthdays in the same order as the props passed
in', () => {
  render(Page, { data: { birthdays } });
  const birthdayEls =
    screen.queryAllByTestId('Birthday');
  expect(birthdayEls[0]).toHaveTextContent(
    /Hercules/
  );
  expect(birthdayEls[1]).toHaveTextContent(
    /Athena/
  );
});
```

3. This will pass, but make sure you verify it doesn't pass by using the same commenting-out trick from previously.

It's also worth pointing out that there is another way to write an ordering test that doesn't involve using the `data-testid` attribute. You could instead get hold of the `ol` element on the page, then map each of the `li` elements to their text content and check that it is an array in the order that you expect.

Dealing with complex props

Sometimes, the props to your component are objects or arrays, and if you were to render them all out within the component stub, you'd end up with a whole bunch of code in the stub. There's a shorter way of outputting prop values, which is to use the `JSON.stringify` function.

Let's do that now for the `BirthdayForm` component:

1. Create a new file named `src/routes/birthdays/__mocks__/BirthdayForm.svelte` with the following content:

```
<script>
  export let form;
</script>

<div>
  Editing {JSON.stringify(form)}
</div>
```

2. In your test suite, add a new call to `vi.mock` that pulls in this component, next to the previous call to `vi.mock`:

```
vi.mock('./BirthdayForm.svelte');
```

3. Next, add the following helper function at the top of the test suite:

```
const firstEditButton = () =>
  screen.queryAllByRole('button', {
    name: 'Edit'
  })[0];
```

4. Then, add the next test, as shown; it also calls `JSON.stringify`. This should pass, but make sure to verify it before finishing:

```
it('passes the currently edited birthday to the BirthdayForm
component', async () => {
  render(Page, { data: { birthdays } });
  await click(firstEditButton());

  expect(
    screen.queryByText(
      `Editing ${JSON.stringify(birthdays[0])}`
    )
  ).toBeInTheDocument();
});
```

You will note the coupling between the component stub and the test suite. This component stub is quite awkward. What I find is that this technique of utilising `JSON.stringify` is generally fine as long as it's the single pattern you use to check complex props and is used consistently between developers.

Dispatching component events

The final component stub technique we will look at is the mechanism to dispatch component events. As in the last section, this is awkward, because it's impossible to raise a component event on a hand-rolled stub without having a dispatcher object defined within the stub itself.

One way to deal with this is to just stick a button into the stub and use that to dispatch the event:

> **Warning**
>
> The following example doesn't make a huge amount of sense in the context of our application: the actual `BirthdayForm` component doesn't have this *cancel* behavior, and if this feature *did* exist, it would probably make more sense to have the **Cancel** button within the page route, avoiding the need for a component event.

1. Update the `BirthdayForm` component stub to include a `button` element that dispatches a `cancel` event:

```
<script>
  import { createEventDispatcher } from 'svelte';
  const dispatcher = createEventDispatcher();
  export let form;
</script>

<div data-testid="BirthdayForm">
  Editing {JSON.stringify(form)}

  <button on:click={() => dispatcher('cancel')} />
</div>
```

2. Now, you can add a test that checks what happens when the `cancel` event is dispatched:

```
it('cancels editing', async () => {
  render(Page, { data: { birthdays } });
  await click(firstEditButton());

  const button = screen
    .getByTestId('BirthdayForm')
    .querySelector('button');

  await click(button);

  expect(
    screen.queryByText(
      `Editing ${JSON.stringify(birthdays[0])}`
    )
  ).not.toBeInTheDocument();
});
```

3. To make this pass, update the `page` component to respond to the `cancel` event:

```
<BirthdayForm
  form={editing}
  on:cancel={() => (editing = null)}
/>
```

Remember, the *real* `BirthdayForm` component doesn't have this behavior, and this exposes a big problem with mocking components: it's challenging to keep the mock aligned with real implementations.

Avoiding hand-rolled mocks and using a library is one way to deal with this problem, as we'll see in the next section.

Using a component mock library

In the last chapter, you saw how you can use `vi.fn` to spy on functions. The `svelte-component-double` npm package can be used in a similar fashion, achieving the same effect as the hand-rolled mocks you've just learned about.

The package includes matchers such as `toBeRendered` and `toBeRenderedWithProps` to check that the component is indeed rendered in the way you wanted.

Let's split this into a couple of parts: installing the library and writing tests.

Installing the library

The library requires a bit of setup to get the relevant matchers into place:

1. Run the following command to install the package:

```
npm install --save-dev svelte-component-double
```

2. Then, create a new file named `src/vitest/registerSvelteComponentDouble.js` with the following content. It registers the matchers and also gives us global access to the `componentDouble` function, which is not required but makes mock setup easier:

```
import { expect } from 'vitest';
import
  as matchers
from 'svelte-component-double/vitest';

expect.extend(matchers);

import {
```

```
      componentDouble
    } from 'svelte-component-double';

    globalThis.componentDouble = componentDouble;
```

3. Then, update your `vite.config.js` file to include the new setup file:

```
    setupFiles: [
      ...,
      './src/vitest/registerSvelteComponentDouble.js'
    ],
```

You're now ready to use the library in your tests.

Writing tests using the componentDouble function

Now, we will rewrite the mock test suite to use the library rather than hand-rolled component stubs:

1. Start by redefining the two calls to `vi.mock` with the following definitions. Each call to `componentDouble` gets a string identifier. This appears in your DOM output and is used in expectation failures:

```
    vi.mock('./Birthday.svelte', async () => ({
      default: componentDouble('Birthday')
    }));
    vi.mock('./BirthdayForm.svelte', async () => ({
      default: componentDouble('BirthdayForm')
    }));
```

2. You'll also need to add two `import` statements at the top of the file so that you can access the mock object. Although it looks like you're importing the actual components, you'll actually get the component doubles:

```
    import Birthday from './Birthday.svelte';
    import BirthdayForm from './BirthdayForm.svelte';
```

3. It's also important to reset the component doubles between each test. That's because `vi.mock` will only generate a double once per test suite. Add the following two calls to `beforeEach` at the top of the `describe` block:

```
    describe('/birthdays', () => {
      beforeEach(Birthday.reset);
      beforeEach(BirthdayForm.reset);
      ...
    });
```

4. You'll also need to update the `import` statement to pull in the `beforeEach` function:

```
import {
  ...,
  beforeEach
} from 'vitest';
```

5. Now for the first test. The makes use of the matcher `toBeRendered`, which checks that the component appears somewhere in the document. Update the first test to look like the following:

```
it('displays a Birthday component for each birthday, () => {
  render(Page, { data: { birthdays } });
  expect(Birthday).toBeRendered();
});
```

6. To run this test, mark it as `it.only` and then run Vitest on this test suite. You should see it passing; you can verify it in the usual way, by commenting out the `Birthday` component instance in the page route component. This time, you'll see a failure printed as follows:

```
Error: Expected "Birthday" component double to be rendered but
it was not
```

7. Undo that change so the test is passing again.

8. We know that not just one `Birthday` is displayed, but two. We can use the `toBeRenderedWithProps` matcher to check for individual instances of the component. Update the same test to use that matcher, like this:

```
it('displays a Birthday component for each birthday', () => {
  render(Page, { data: { birthdays } });
  expect(Birthday).toBeRenderedWithProps({
    name: 'Hercules',
    dob: '1994-02-02'
  });
  expect(Birthday).toBeRenderedWithProps({
    name: 'Athena',
    dob: '1989-01-01'
  });
});
```

Notice how the calls to `toBeRenderedWithProps` do not need to specify the full set of props. If the given subset matches, the expectation passes. That means we can avoid checking the `id` field, which is unnecessary detail for the purposes of this test.

9. If you comment out the rendering of `Birthday` in the component, you'll see what a failure for this matcher looks like:

    ```
    Error: Expected "Birthday" component double to have been
    rendered once with props but it was not

    Expected: Object {
      "dob": "1994-02-02",
      "name": "Hercules",
    }
    Received:
    ```

10. The second test in this test suite checks the ordering of components. We can do that with the library by using the `propsOfAllInstances` function that exists on the double. Update the test to read as follows:

    ```
    it('displays the Birthdays in the same order as the props passed
    in', () => {
      render(Page, { data: { birthdays } });
      expect(Birthday.propsOfAllInstances()).toEqual([
        expect.objectContaining({ name: 'Hercules' }),
        expect.objectContaining({ name: 'Athena' })
      ]);
    });
    ```

11. The first test for `BirthdayForm` no longer needs any `JSON.stringify` magic. We can just test the object prop directly. Update the test as follows:

    ```
    it('passes the currently edited birthday to the BirthdayForm
    component', async () => {
      render(Page, { data: { birthdays } });
      await click(firstEditButton());

      expect(BirthdayForm).toBeRenderedWithProps({
        form: birthdays[0]
      });
    });
    ```

12. And finally, the last test can make use of the `dispatch` double function to dispatch an event to the parent component. Note how much simpler this is than the hand-rolled mock:

    ```
    it('cancels editing', async () => {
      render(Page, { data: { birthdays } });
      await click(firstEditButton());

      await BirthdayForm.dispatch('cancel');
    ```

```
    expect(BirthdayForm).not.toBeRenderedWithProps({
      form: birthdays[0]
    });
  });
```

These last two tests show how much simpler it can be to use a component mock library over hand-rolled mocks. That completes this section. You've now discovered all there is to using the `svelte-component-double` library to simplify your test suites.

Summary

This chapter has taken a very detailed look at component mocks. We started by looking at how it's often possible to avoid using component mocks in the majority of cases, which is important because component mocks are a big cause of complexity in test suites.

You then saw how to use hand-rolled mocks that take advantage of Vitest's `vi.mock` function together with component stubs in the specially named `__mocks__` directory. You also saw how they can quickly become complex.

Finally, we looked at using the `svelte-component-double` library to avoid using hand-rolled mocks. This provides a couple of simple matchers together with some helper functions to assist you in writing tests.

That completes all the unit testing topics within this book. The next chapter adds one more testing technique: using Cucumber.js to write **Behavior-Driven Development** (**BDD**) style tests for your team.

13

Adding Cucumber Tests

Up until now, you have seen two types of automated tests: Vitest unit tests and Playwright end-to-end tests. This chapter adds a third type of test: **Cucumber** (https://cucumber.io).

Just like Playwright, Cucumber has its own test runner, which is typically set up to drive your application in the same way as Playwright does. The difference is that Cucumber tests are not written in JavaScript code.

Cucumber tests are contained within *feature files* that contain tests formatted in a special syntax known as **Gherkin**. These tests, known as **features** and organized into scenarios, read like plain English. That has a couple of advantages.

First, they can be written and understood by the whole team, not just developers. That means you can extend test-first practices outside of the development team.

Second, the absence of code encourages you to write tests that focus on user behavior rather than the technical details of the software. That, in turn, encourages you to build the right thing for your users.

How does Cucumber turn features into executable code? Well, take a look at an example line (or, step) from a feature file:

```
When I navigate to the "/birthdays" page
```

Cucumber takes this step and looks for a matching JavaScript-defined step definition. The step definition, in this case, looks like this:

```
When(
  'I navigate to the {string} page',
  async function (url) { ... }
);
```

Notice that the step definition has an associated code block. Once Cucumber finds a matching step definition, it executes that code block, supplying any parsed arguments. In this case, the url parameter will be provided as the /birthdays string. Cucumber also supports other data types, such as int and bigdecimal (https://github.com/cucumber/cucumber-expressions#parameter-types).

We will cover the following key topics in this chapter:

- Creating the feature file

- Setting up a Playwright world object

- Implementing step definitions

By the end of the chapter, you'll be confident in adding Cucumber tests to your application.

Technical requirements

The code for the chapter can be found online at `https://github.com/PacktPublishing/Svelte-with-Test-Driven-Development/tree/main/Chapter13/Start`.

Creating the feature file

We begin with writing an example Cucumber feature file.

The Gherkin syntax that's used to write features is characterized by the three words *Given*, *When*, and *Then*. These are analogous to the *Arrange*, *Act*, and *Assert* sections of all good unit tests, so they should feel familiar.

Let's jump right in with our feature file and see what happens when we execute the test:

1. Start by adding a new directory, `features`, with a new `features/birthdays.feature` file with the following content. It describes a user scenario in which the *Birthdays* application already supports editing a birthday. Here it is:

```
Feature: Editing a birthday
  Scenario: Correcting the year of birth
    Given An existing birthday for "Hercules" on
      "1992-03-04"
    When I navigate to the "/birthdays" page
    And I edit the birthday for "Hercules" to be
      "1994-04-06"
    Then the birthday for "Hercules" should show
      "1994-04-06"
    And the text "1992-03-04" should not appear on the
      page
```

2. Install Cucumber using the following command:

```
npm install --save-dev @cucumber/cucumber
```

3. Then, go ahead and run the test with `npx @cucumber/cucumber`. You should see an output that starts like this:

```
Failures:

1) Scenario: Correcting the year of birth #
      features/birthdays.feature:2
   ? Given An existing birthday for "Hercules" on
     "1992-03-04"
   Undefined. Implement with the following snippet:

   Given('An existing birthday for {string} on
   {string}', function (string, string2) {
       // Write code here that turns the phrase above
           into concrete actions
       return 'pending';
   });
```

Just as all good test runners should, Cucumber is telling us the next task: defining the step definition. But before we get there, we need to pull in the Playwright APIs.

Setting up a Playwright world object

How does Cucumber execute your test? Just like with the Playwright tests, we need a running application server and a running browser to drive the **user interface** (**UI**). In this section, we'll write all the code that gets the environment ready for test execution.

Cucumber.js uses the concept of a **world object** that describes the contextual information that is shared between each scenario step. This is an object that is bound to the `this` variable in each step. We also get access to it in special `Before` and `After` hooks, which are run before and after each scenario.

The world object should contain functions (and state) that allow you to drive the UI. Since you've already learned and used the Playwright API for locating objects on a page, it would be marvelous if we could use that same API. It turns out we can indeed do this. We can also use the same `expect` API we're used to as well, and we'll do that in the next section when we begin writing step definitions.

Here's what we'll do: we'll build a world class named `PlaywrightWorld` that has the following functions:

*   `launchServer` and `killServer` for starting and stopping the server
*   `launchBrowser` and `closeBrowser` for opening and closing a headless web browser, and for exposing the Playwright page and `request` APIs on our world object

Then, we'll use the `Before` and `After` hooks to start and stop both the server and browser.

One final note before we begin: our code files will use the mjs extension rather than js, to signify to Cucumber.js that these files use ECMAScript Module syntax.

Let's begin:

1. Start by creating a new file, features/support/world.mjs, with the following import definitions. We'll add more later, but these are enough to get us started with launching the server:

```
import * as childProcess from 'child_process';
import {
  setWorldConstructor
} from '@cucumber/cucumber';
```

2. Now, define the removeAnsiColorCodes function. This is important for execution environments (Windows, primarily) that will return color codes in the stdout stream data:

```
const removeAnsiColorCodes = (string) =>
  string.replace(/\x1b\[[0-9;]+m/g, '');
```

3. We're ready to define the PlaywrightWorld class, starting with a single method, launchServer. That method ends with a call to setWorldConstructor that makes this the designated world class:

```
class PlaywrightWorld {
  async launchServer() {
    console.log('launching server');
    this.serverProcess = childProcess.spawn(
      config.webServer.command,
      [],
      { shell: true, env: config.webServer.env }
    );
    this.baseUrl = await new Promise((resolve) => {
      this.serverProcess.stdout.on('data', (data) => {
      let text = removeAnsiColorCodes(String(data));
      let match = text.match(
        /http[s]?:\/\/[a-z]+:[0-9]+\//
      );
      if (match) {
        resolve(match[0]);
      }
    });
    console.log(`started at ${this.baseUrl}`);
  }
}

setWorldConstructor(PlaywrightWorld);
```

The code in our `launchServer` function is very crude, but it does the job. It reads the Playwright configuration file and pulls out the value of `config.webServer.command`, which on my project is this:

```
npm run build && npm run preview
```

Launching the web server using Playwright config

Because this is a shell command, we must use the `detached` and `shell` properties when calling Node's `childProcess.spawn` function.

Setting `env` means that any environment variables that Cucumber receives are also passed to this new shell. Once the server is started, we read the `stdout` data stream until we see a line that contains an HTTP URL. This is the URL of our running web server, so we parse that value and return it as the argument to `resolve`.

The use of the `Promise` object means that the thread will wait until the value is retrieved, and then set the world's `baseUrl` property to this value.

---

4. Add the following error handling logic, which simply logs out any non-empty messages that appear on the `stderr` data stream:

```
class PlaywrightWorld {
  async launchServer() {
    console.log('launching server');
    this.serverProcess = childProcess.spawn(...);
    this.serverProcess.stderr.on('data', (data) => {
      const trimmed = String(data).trim();
      if (trimmed !== '') {
        console.log(trimmed);
      }
    });
    ...
    console.log(`started at ${this.baseUrl}`);
  }
```

5. Now let's move on to `killServer`, starting by adding a new package, `tree-kill-promise`, that will allow us to easily shut down the server process:

```
npm install --save-dev tree-kill-promise
```

6. Then add that as an import at the top of the same world file:

```
import kill from 'tree-kill-promise';
```

7. Define the `killServer` method, shown here:

```
class PlaywrightWorld {
  ...
  killServer() {
    await kill(this.serverProcess.pid);
  }
}
```

8. It's time to launch the browser. Start by bringing in the following Playwright `import` statements at the top of the file:

```
import { chromium, request } from '@playwright/test';
```

9. Then define the `launchBrowser` and `closeBrowser` functions, as shown in the following code. The crucial piece is that we then end up with the `request` and `page` objects, which are the exact same objects we have in our Playwright end-to-end tests:

```
class PlaywrightWorld {
  ...
  async launchBrowser() {
    this.browser = await chromium.launch();
    this.context = await this.browser.newContext({
      baseURL: this.baseUrl
    });
    this.request = await request.newContext({
      baseURL: `${this.baseUrl}api/`
    });
    this.page = await this.context.newPage();
  }

  async closeBrowser() {
    await this.browser.close();
  }
}
```

10. With the world object complete, it's time for the hooks. Add a new file named `features/support/hooks.mjs` and give it the following content:

```
import { Before, After } from '@cucumber/cucumber';

Before(async function () {
  await this.launchServer();
  await this.launchBrowser();
});
```

```
After(async function () {
  await this.killServer();
  this.closeBrowser();
});
```

That's all the setup complete. The only remaining thing is the step definitions.

Implementing the step definitions

The final piece of the puzzle is the Given, When, and Then functions for matching feature steps with their implementations.

> **Checking your work as you go along**
>
> In this section we will speed through the definition, but make sure you verify each step is working by running Cucumber (with the npx @cucumber/cucumber command) after you've implemented each function.

Let's do it!

1. Create another new directory, features/support, and create a file named features/support/steps.mjs, which starts with the following imports:

    ```
    import {
      Given,
      When,
      Then
    } from '@cucumber/cucumber';
    ```

2. Then implement the first Given step from our feature file. This one calls into the API using the this.request.post function from Playwright. Note the use of failOnStatusCode, which makes sure that Cucumber fails the test if we don't get a 200 OK response back:

    ```
    Given(
      'An existing birthday for {string} on {string}',
      async function (name, dob) {
        await this.request.post('birthdays', {
          data: { name, dob },
          failOnStatusCode: true
        });
      }
    );
    ```

3. Now we're on to the When steps. There are two of these; arguably, one could have been `Given`, but I think they work nicely as a group, given that they are both user actions. The first one simply calls `this.page.goto`, which you've also seen before:

```
When(
  'I navigate to the {string} page',
  async function (url) {
    await this.page.goto(url);
  }
);
```

4. For the remaining steps, we will use our own `BirthdayListPage` page model object that we defined in *Chapter 7, Tidying up Test Suites*. Start by importing that at the top of the file:

```
import {
  BirthdayListPage
} from '../../tests/BirthdayListPage.js';
```

5. Then implement the next When step definition, which uses our battled-tested `beginEditingFor`, `dateOfBirthField`, and `saveButton` functions:

```
When(
  'I edit the birthday for {string} to be {string}',
  async function (name, dob) {
    const birthdayListPage = new BirthdayListPage(
      this.page
    );
    await birthdayListPage.beginEditingFor(name);
    await birthdayListPage
      .dateOfBirthField()
      .fill(dob);
    await birthdayListPage.saveButton().click();
  }
);
```

6. It's time for the Then step definitions. These are the ones that have expectations. To begin, add an `import` statement for `expect` at the top of the file:

```
import { expect } from '@playwright/test';
```

7. Implement the first Then clause, shown in the following code block. This checks that the new birthday is shown on the page:

```
Then(
  'the birthday for {string} should show {string}',
  async function (name, dob) {
    const birthdayListPage = new BirthdayListPage(
      this.page
    );
    await expect(
      birthdayListPage.entryFor(name)
    ).toContainText(dob);
  }
);
```

8. Complete the step definitions with the final Then clause:

```
Then(
  'the text {string} should not appear on the page',
  async function (text) {
    await expect(
      this.page.getByText(text)
    ).not.toBeVisible();
  }
);
```

9. Running the tests now, you should see all of them passing:

```
work/birthdays % npx @cucumber/cucumber
launching server
started at http://localhost:4173/
.......

1 scenario (1 passed)
5 steps (5 passed)
```

You've now seen how to write a feature file using the Gherkin syntax, and how to write step definitions that use the same Playwright API that you've been using for your end-to-end-tests. You've also seen that the standard expect syntax can be used to write assertions that is used across all three types of tests.

Summary

This chapter covered how to use the Cucumber test runner to execute Gherkin feature files. Gherkin's plain-English syntax makes this an important technique for bringing automated testing to the wider product development team.

The feature files are backed by step definitions. These step definitions are implemented using the `Given`, `When`, and `Then` functions, which map Gherkin step descriptions to JavaScript code.

You've seen how step definitions can re-use the existing Playwright API code to manage browser interactions.

This completes our look at automated testing techniques. In *Part 3*, we'll look at how to write unit tests for SvelteKit-specific features, starting with a chapter on strategies for testing authentication.

Part 3: Testing SvelteKit Features

This part takes a glance at some specific features that require careful testing. These chapters aren't sequential as in the previous parts. Instead, they are discussions on how you might approach your testing. The code samples included focus only on the novel pieces that haven't been covered in previous chapters. You can always refer to the online repository for complete implementations.

This part has the following chapters:

- *Chapter 14, Testing Authentication*
- *Chapter 15, Test-Driving Svelte Stores*
- *Chapter 16, Test-Driving Service Workers*

Testing Authentication

Many web applications will involve authenticating users. This chapter shows how you can write tests for this functionality. These tests cover logging in, logging out, and ensuring that your application is only accessible to logged-in users.

This chapter is not a walkthrough and only includes a small amount of detail on the application code required to implement authentication. The book repository uses the **Auth.js** library, but the same testing techniques will work regardless of the implementation approach.

The chapter covers the following key topics:

- Testing authentication with Playwright
- Testing authentication with Vitest

By the end of the chapter, you'll have seen how to write tests that cover all aspects of authentication.

Technical requirements

The code for the chapter can be found online at `https://github.com/PacktPublishing/Svelte-with-Test-Driven-Development/tree/main/Chapter14/Complete`.

If you want to run the code in this sample, you'll need to create a `.env` file with some environment variables. There's an example file named `.env.example` that you can copy and save as `.env`, which should work, but if you want to try the GitHub OAuth integration, you'll need to do some configuration within GitHub.

You'll find more detailed information in the repository's `README.md` file.

Testing authentication with Playwright

This section details the groundwork required for effective testing with your Playwright tests. First, we look at how to provide hard-coded authentication credentials for your end-to-end tests. Then we use this to verify that users can log in and log out of the application. Finally, we'll update the existing tests so that they ensure the user is logged in before attempting to test the application functionality.

> **What about Cucumber?**
>
> If you're using Cucumber tests with Playwright, then the same techniques presented here will also work for you.

Creating an auth profile for dev and test modes

It's fairly typical to use OAuth authentication strategies that delegate authentication responsibilities to a third-party provider, such as Google or GitHub. However, when it comes to writing end-to-end tests, it's impractical to maintain user accounts with these third parties just for the purposes of testing. For one thing, account passwords expire and need to be reset periodically. And that kind of work needs to be documented, tracked and scheduled.

Another solution is to provide a special hard-coded credential that can be used to log in when the application server is run in a specific test mode. Your Playwright tests can then use this credential to log in.

Our solution does this in the following way:

1. Playwright starts the server with an additional environment variable, `VITE_ALLOW_CREDENTIALS`, that is set to `true`.

2. The `Auth.js` initialization code looks for this credential, and, if it is found, enables login via its credentials mechanism. There is a single user, `api`, which has no password associated with it.

3. This user can then be used by both the API tests and your application dev mode.

To ensure Playwright starts with the right environment variable, the `playwright.config.js` file changes like this:

```
webServer: {
  command:
    'npm run build && npm run preview',
  port: 4173,
  env: {
    PATH: process.env.PATH,
    VITE_ALLOW_CREDENTIALS: true
  }
},
```

Then, the application has a file named `src/authProviders.js` that checks for the credential, shown in the following code snippet. This sample is specific to `Auth.js`, but other authentication libraries can be initialized similarly. The key point is that the expected `authProviders` is an array that may or may not contain the special credentials provider, depending on the value of the environment variable:

```
import GitHubProvider from '@auth/core/providers/github';
import CredentialsProvider from '@auth/core/providers/credentials';
import {
  GITHUB_ID,
  GITHUB_SECRET
} from '$env/static/private';

const allowCredentials =
  import.meta.env.VITE_ALLOW_CREDENTIALS === 'true';

const GitHub = GitHubProvider({
  clientId: GITHUB_ID,
  clientSecret: GITHUB_SECRET
});

const credentials = CredentialsProvider({
  credentials: {
    username: { label: 'Username', type: 'text' }
  },
  async authorize({ username }, req) {
    if (username === 'api')
      return { id: '1', name: 'api' };
  }
});

const devAuthProviders = {
  GitHub,
  credentials
};

const prodAuthProviders = { GitHub };

export const authProviders = allowCredentials
  ? devAuthProviders
  : prodAuthProviders;
```

With the application primed, it's ready to be used in our tests.

Writing tests for login

It's important to have one test for a successful login flow and one for an unsuccessful one. Having these tests ensures you have automated test coverage of these pages.

Here's an example of a successful login test. It can be found in the `tests/login.test.js` repository file. It navigates to the usual `/birthdays` route, then looks for a button named **credentials**. It clicks that, fills in the magic `api` user, and clicks the button again (which, this time, acts to submit the login information). It then checks that the user has been redirected to the main page and can see the **Birthday list** heading:

```js
import { expect, test } from '@playwright/test';

test('logs in and returns to the application', async ({
  page
}) => {
  await page.goto('/birthdays');

  await page.waitForLoadState('networkidle');

  await page
    .getByRole('button', { name: /Sign in with
      credentials/i })
    .click();

  await page.getByRole('textbox').fill('api');

  await page
    .getByRole('button', { name: /Sign in with
      credentials/i })
    .click();

  await expect(
    page.getByText('Birthday list')
  ).toBeVisible();
});
```

Note the use of the `page.waitForLoadState` Playwright function. This is necessary to ensure that all the relevant `Auth.js` code has run and eventually renders the sign-in button.

Next is the test for an unsuccessful login. For this, we can give any username other than `api`, so this test supplies the `unknown user` text, which gives the data some useful context:

```
test('does not log in if log in fails', async ({
  page
}) => {
  await page.goto('/birthdays');

  await expect(
    page.getByText('Please login')
  ).toBeVisible();

  await page.waitForLoadState('networkidle');

  await page
    .getByRole('button', { name: /Sign in with
      credentials/i })
    .click();

  await page
    .getByRole('textbox')
    .fill('unknown user');

  await page
    .getByRole('button', { name: /Sign in with
      credentials/i })
    .click();

  await expect(
    page.getByText(
      'Sign in failed. Check the details you provided are
        correct.'
    )
  ).toBeVisible();
});
```

That covers the tests for the new login functionality. Next, we need to update existing tests to ensure they continue to work.

Updating existing tests to authenticate the user

The existing tests we have in `tests/birthdays.test.js` need to be updated so that each test starts with a logged-in user. We can do this using a `beforeEach` block, which has the advantage that the original tests doesn't need to be modified.

Auth.js provides a neat API-like endpoint that we can call directly. This means that we don't need to navigate through the web form for each test, which reduces the amount of work each test needs to do.

The `login` function is defined in the following code snippet. It mimics the action of clicking the **Sign in** button that submits the login form. First, it retrieves a **Cross-Site Request Forgery (CSRF)** token and then submits a form response with the CSRF token attached and a `username` field value of `api`. It's also important to send the `origin` header with this request; otherwise, it will be rejected:

```
const login = async ({ context, baseURL }) => {
  const response = await context.request.get(
    '/auth/csrf'
  );
  const { csrfToken } = await response.json();
  const response2 = await context.request.post(
    '/auth/callback/credentials',
    {
      form: {
        username: 'api',
        csrfToken
      },
      headers: {
        origin: baseURL
      }
    }
  );
};
```

That can then be triggered for each test in `tests/birthday.test.js` by sending it to `test.beforeEach`, like this:

```
test.beforeEach(login);
```

That completes the Playwright tests. You'll note I've left out any test to check what happens when you go to the `/birthday` route in an unauthenticated state. We'll cover that in the Vitest tests in the next section.

Testing authentication with Vitest

Now we drop down a level and get into specifics. Our tests will focus on the `/birthdays` route and how it is presented given authentication data.

The Auth.js library utilizes SvelteKit's session mechanism for passing authentication information into components, so what we do is harness that via the `parent.session` object and the `locals.getSession` function. All we have to do is use test doubles to mimic the responses we want.

We start by defining a session factory that can be used to set up these session test doubles. Then we'll update page load tests with new authentication functionality, and finally, we'll end with updating the form action tests.

Defining a session factory

Here's the definition of `src/factories/session.js`, which defines four exports that are used in the subsequent tests:

```
import { vi } from 'vitest';

const validSession = { user: 'api ' };

export const loggedInSession = () => ({
  session: validSession
});

export const loggedOutSession = () => ({
  session: null
});

export const loggedInLocalsSession = () => ({
  getSession: vi.fn().mockResolvedValue(validSession)
});

export const loggedOutLocalsSession = () => ({
  getSession: vi.fn().mockResolvedValue(null)
});
```

A `loggedInSession` object can be used as the `parent` property that's passed to your page load. The Auth.js authentication process will run before your route is loaded and merged into this `parent` value. So, `loggedInSession` is just a dummy object: in the context of our tests, any value at all constitutes a valid, logged-in user.

The `loggedOutSession` object is similar: this time, a `null` value for `session` means that the user is not authenticated.

The `loggedInLocalsSession` and `loggedOutLocalsSession` values are to be used in place of SvelteKit's `locals` property that is passed to your form action. This property is a collection of functions that the form action can make use of.

Next, we'll see how to make use of these tests.

Updating existing tests for page load functions

Now let's update the page load function so that it has the necessary load function. We'll also write a test to ensure that the page does *not* load any data if the user is not authenticated.

There's a new import needed in `src/routes/birthdays/page.server.test.js`, shown in the following code block. These are the two factories that will be used to provide values for the `parent` property passed to the `load` function:

```
import {
  loggedInSession,
  loggedOutSession,
} from 'src/factories/session.js';
```

Then, the `describe` block is updated to create a `parent` variable that is defaulted to a logged-in user:

```
describe('/birthdays - load', () => {
  const parent = vi.fn();

  beforeEach(() => {
    parent.mockResolvedValue(loggedInSession());
  });

  ...
});
```

Each of the tests also needs to be updated to pass this new `parent` property into the `load` function:

```
it('calls fetch with /api/birthdays', async () => {
  const fetch = vi.fn();
  fetch.mockResolvedValue(fetchResponseOk());
  const result = await load({ fetch, parent });
  expect(fetch).toBeCalledWith('/api/birthdays');
});
```

You'll also want to add a test to check that the endpoint won't work without the correct authentication. In the following example, we override the default `parent` property with `loggedOutSession` and then test that the returned page has a 303 status, meaning the browser is being redirected. It also checks the page being redirected to is the `/login` route:

```
it('redirects if the request is not authorised', async () => {
  parent.mockResolvedValue(loggedOutSession());
  expect.hasAssertions();
  try {
    await load({ parent });
  } catch (error) {
```

```
    expect(error.status).toEqual(303);
    expect(error.location).toEqual('/login');
  }
});
```

That completes the tests for the `load` function.

Updating existing tests for form actions

For the form action tests, the `import` statement is updated with the remaining two factory functions:

```
import {
  loggedInSession,
  loggedOutSession,
  loggedInLocalsSession,
  loggedOutLocalsSession
} from 'src/factories/session.js';
```

Then, the `describe` block is updated to include a `locals` variable that is set within `beforeEach`. Note that this time the variable is defined as `let` because the `loggedInLocalsSession` factory is responsible for setting up the `vi.fn` spy function:

```
describe('/birthdays - default action', () => {
  const fetch = vi.fn();
  let locals;

  beforeEach(() => {
    fetch.mockResolvedValue(fetchResponseOk());
    locals = loggedInLocalsSession();
  });


  ...
});
```

Then `performFormAction` changes to include the `locals` property. Since this is the function that our tests call to invoke the form action, none of the tests themselves need to change:

```
const performFormAction = (formData) =>
  actions.default({
    request: createFormDataRequest(formData),
    fetch,
    locals
  });
```

Finally, we need a test to check what happens if the form is submitted when the user is not authenticated. In this case, we return a 300 status code rather than a redirect, but you could choose to go back to the previous form page, as you would with a validation error. That would help in the scenario where the user's session has expired. Here's the simpler version:

```
describe('when not authorised', () => {
  beforeEach(() => {
    locals = loggedOutLocalsSession();
  });

  it('returns a failure', async () => {
    const result = await performFormAction({});
    expect(result.status).toEqual(300);
  });
});
```

That completes the Vitest changes required to support our authentication implementation.

Summary

This chapter briefly looked at the kinds of tests you'll need for testing authentication.

Playwright end-to-end tests should check the login flows, both successful and unsuccessful. They should also make use of fake credentials where possible and ensure that any routes are accessible only by authenticated users who are logged in using a test.beforeEach call.

Vitest tests for authenticated routes work differently. They focus on the session object that SvelteKit returns: does it have a valid value or not?

While this covers the basics, most applications will have much more complex needs: for example, your application might have individual data stores for each user, not just one global data store such as our Birthdays application.

The Playwright website contains good documentation on how to test specific patterns, such as having multiple user roles interact within one test. That can be found at https://playwright.dev/docs/auth.

In the next chapter, we'll look at testing Svelte Stores.

15

Test-Driving Svelte Stores

Stores are a useful mechanism for sharing state that exists outside of the normal Svelte component hierarchy. You can think of stores as global variables but with a protective mechanism – the `subscribe` mechanism – that helps ensure that all components maintain a consistent view of each variable's current value.

When it comes to writing tests for components that involve stores, you've got to write tests for two halves: the first half for the *observation* of the store value and the second half for the *setting* of the store value.

Because stores are an internal design decision, there's no need to write a Playwright test specifically for the introduction of stores.

This chapter covers the following key topics:

- Designing a store for birthdays
- Writing tests for reading store values
- Writing tests for updating store values

By the end of the chapter, you'll have a good understanding of writing unit tests for Svelte store objects.

Technical requirements

The code for the chapter can be found online at `https://github.com/PacktPublishing/Svelte-with-Test-Driven-Development/tree/main/Chapter15/Complete`.

Designing a store for birthdays

The code for this chapter includes a single store in the `src/stores/birthdays.js` file with the following content:

```
import { writable } from 'svelte/store';

export const birthdays = writable([]);
```

The idea of the `birthdays` store is to store whatever birthdays have been returned from the SvelteKit page load. It's kept up to date by the page route component.

There's also a new `NextBirthday` component that reads the store and displays a message at the top of the page alerting the user to the next upcoming birthday.

> **Stores aren't necessary for this change**
>
> This feature could have been written simply by passing `birthdays` as a prop to `NextBirthday`. It's certainly worth avoiding stores if you can simply use component props. This chapter's code is intended to be educative only; in reality I would not use a store for this use case.

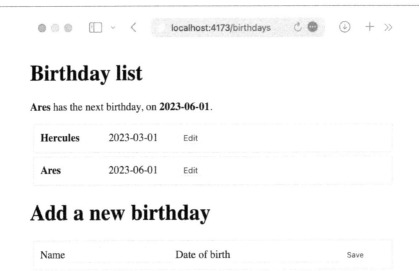

Figure 15.1 – The Birthdays application with the new alert

The code for the `NextBirthday` component is not trivial, so you may be interested in checking it out online. In particular, the unit tests make use of the `vi.useFakeTimers` and `vi.setSystemTime` functions to ensure that the test checks aren't affected by the passing of real time.

That's all the design necessary. Let's look at the tests.

Writing tests for reading store values

There are at least two tests needed when reading the store value: first, for the initial value when the component loads, and second, when an update comes in.

Here's an example of the first, which you'll find in `src/routes/birthdays/NextBirthday.test.js`. Notice how we import the `birthdays` store with the name, `birthdaysStore`, which makes it very clear in the test that the object imported is the store. The *Arrange* phase of the test then calls `birthdayStore.set` to prime the store with its initial value before the component is mounted:

```
import {
  birthdays as birthdaysStore
} from '../../stores/birthdays.js';


...

describe('NextBirthday', () => {
  it('displays a single birthday', () => {
    birthdaysStore.set([
      createBirthday('Hercules', '2023-09-01')
    ]);
    render(NextBirthday);
    expect(document.body).toHaveTextContent(
      'Hercules has the next birthday, on 2056-09-01'
    );
  });
});
```

You may be curious why the year `2056` is mentioned in the expectation. That's because we used `vi.setSystemTime` to set the current date to a fixed date:

```
const julyOfYear = (year) => {
  const date = new Date();
  date.setFullYear(year, 6, 1);
  return date;
};

describe('NextBirthday', () => {
  beforeEach(() => {
    vi.useFakeTimers();
    vi.setSystemTime(julyOfYear(2056));
  });

  afterEach(() => {
```

```
    vi.useRealTimers();
  });


  ...

});
```

The second test has the same initial setting, but now the `render` call moves into the *Arrange* phase, and the *Act* phase is now a second call to `birthdayStore.set`. Notice also that this call needs to be marked with `await` so that the component has the opportunity to re-render:

```
it('updates the displayed data when the store is updated', async () =>
{
  birthdaysStore.set([
    createBirthday('Hercules', '2023-09-01')
  ]);
  render(NextBirthday);
  await birthdaysStore.set([
    createBirthday('Hercules', '2023-09-01'),
    createBirthday('Ares', '2023-08-01')
  ]);
  expect(document.body).toHaveTextContent(
    'Ares has the next birthday, on 2056-08-01'
  );
});
```

This test will only pass if the component is set to observe the store. You can see this in `src/routes/birthdays/NextBirthday.svelte`:

```
$: nextBirthday = findNextBirthday($birthdays);
```

The test would fail if the argument to the function was `birthdays` and not `$birthdays`.

Next, let's look at the tests for setting the value.

Writing tests for updating store values

The page route component is responsible for ensuring the birthdays that are passed into it are saved in the store.

Here's the first test from the `src/routes/birthdays/page.test.js` file, which uses `birthdaysStore.subscribe` to set a `storedBirthdays` value within the test. After rendering the component, it expects the `storedBirthdays` value to contain the birthdays:

```
it('saves the loaded birthdays into the birthdays store', () => {
  let storedBirthdays;
```

```
birthdaysStore.subscribe(
    (value) => (storedBirthdays = value)
);
render(Page, { data: { birthdays } });
expect(storedBirthdays).toEqual(birthdays);
});
```

A second test is then needed to ensure the store value is updated whenever the component prop changes. This test makes use of the $set function on the returned component to update the props on the component:

```
it('updates the birthdays store when the component props change',
async () => {
  let storedBirthdays;
  birthdaysStore.subscribe(
    (value) => (storedBirthdays = value)
  );
  const { component } = render(Page, {
    data: { birthdays }
  });
  await component.$set({ data: { birthdays: [] } });
  expect(storedBirthdays).toEqual([]);
});
```

And that's all there is to it.

Summary

This short chapter covered some important concepts for testing Svelte stores: first, how to test the two halves of observing and setting Svelte store values, and second, how you can rename the store import so that it's more readable within your tests. In our case, that meant renaming birthdays as birthdaysStore.

You've also seen how to call the store's set and subscribe methods within your tests, and how to use Svelte's $set function on the component instance to update props to a previously rendered component.

Taken together, these techniques highlight how advanced Svelte features are still testable at the unit level if that's desired. Of course, you might get just as much value from writing Playwright tests that can happily ignore the internal mechanics of Svelte stores.

The next chapter covers a more complicated topic: **service workers**.

16

Test-Driving Service Workers

This chapter looks at **service workers**, which are bits of code that are installed on the browser and are invoked before any HTTP operation. That makes them useful for a certain set of features, such as enabling offline access to your app. The service worker implemented in this chapter provides exactly that feature.

It's almost always a good idea to use off-the-shelf service workers rather than rolling your own. But it's instructive to see how you might test your own service workers, hence the inclusion in this book.

The term **testability** is used to describe how straightforward it is to write tests for your application code. The way we structure our components and modules has a big impact on their testability. Service workers are a great example of taking something that, at first glance, is a highly complex thing to test and restructuring its implementation so that the tests become almost trivial.

This chapter covers the following key topics:

- Adding a Playwright test for offline access
- Implementing the service worker

By the end of the chapter, you'll have learned how to test-drive service workers, plus you'll have learned a new technique for making your application code more testable.

Technical requirements

The code for the chapter can be found online at `https://github.com/PacktPublishing/Svelte-with-Test-Driven-Development/tree/main/Chapter16/Complete`.

Adding a Playwright test for offline access

Service workers tend to have a specific intent. In our case, the service worker enables the application to be used offline: loading the application causes it to be cached. If the network is no longer accessible, the next page load will be served from this cache, courtesy of the service worker.

Therefore, the Playwright test needs to test the application's behavior when there's no network connection.

At the time of writing, Playwright's support for service worker events is experimental, so it needs to be enabled using the PW_EXPERIMENTAL_SERVICE_WORKER_NETWORK_EVENTS flag in your package.json file:

```
{
  "scripts": {
    ...,
    "test": "PW_EXPERIMENTAL_SERVICE_WORKER_NETWORK_EVENTS=1
      playwright test",
    ...
    }
}
```

Once that's done, we're ready to write our tests. We need two helper functions. The first, waitForServiceWorkerActivation, can be invoked by any Playwright test to ensure that subsequent commands don't run until the service worker is actively caching new requests.

This code can be found in tests/offline.test.js. I've parked it right next to the single test that uses it: there's not much point in moving it to another file because I don't expect to reuse this function anywhere else in the test suite:

```
const waitForServiceWorkerActivation = (page) =>
  page.evaluate(async () => {
    const registration =
      await
        window.navigator.serviceWorker.getRegistration();
    if (registration.active?.state === 'activated')
      return;
    await new Promise((res) =>
      window.navigator.serviceWorker.addEventListener(
        'controllerchange',
        res
      )
    );
  });
```

Next, we need a disableNetwork function that will cause any network request to return a network error:

```
const disableNetwork = (context) =>
  context.route('', (route) => route.abort());
```

Then we're ready to write the test:

```
test('site is available offline', async ({
  page,
  context,
  browser
}) => {
  await page.goto('/birthdays');

  await waitForServiceWorkerActivation(page);
  await disableNetwork(context);

  await page.goto('/birthdays');

  await expect(
    page.getByText('Birthday list')
  ).toBeVisible();
});
```

Without the service worker, this test will fail because the second `page.goto` call will error. In the next section, we'll see how this service worker can be implemented.

Implementing the service worker

Service workers have an odd interface. For one thing, they need to rely on a variable named `self` that is provided by the browser context. Then they need to attach listeners to certain events, and they need to use the `event.waitUntil` function to ensure that the browser waits for its operations to finish before assuming the worker is ready.

It turns out that it's quite difficult to set up a value for `self` together with fake events within your Vitest tests. Not impossible, but difficult and laborious.

Given this complexity, the trick to implementing a testable service worker is to move most of the functionality into another module: each event becomes a simple function call, and we can test that function call rather than the event.

Then, we leave the service worker module untested. We still have the Playwright test giving us coverage, and this code isn't likely to change once it's complete, so it's no big deal that this particular file is without unit tests.

This example, shown in the following code block, is stored in the `src/service-worker.js` file. It pushes almost all the functionality into the `addFilesToCache`, `deleteOldCaches`, and `fetchWithCacheOnError` functions:

```js
import {
  build,
  files,
  version
} from '$service-worker';
import {
  addFilesToCache,
  deleteOldCaches,
  fetchWithCacheOnError
} from './lib/service-worker.js';

const cacheId = `cache-${version}`;
const appFiles = ['/birthdays'];
const assets = [...build, ...files, ...appFiles];

self.addEventListener('install', (event) => {
  event.waitUntil(addFilesToCache(cacheId, assets));
});

self.addEventListener('activate', (event) => {
  event.waitUntil(deleteOldCaches(cacheId));
  event.waitUntil(self.clients.claim());
});

self.addEventListener('fetch', (event) => {
  if (event.request.method !== 'GET') return;

  event.respondWith(
    fetchWithCacheOnError(cacheId, event.request)
  );
});
```

Let's take a look at the implementation of the three functions located in the `src/lib/service-worker.js` file. Each of these functions makes use of the Cache API, which we'll test by setting up spies.

Here's `addFilesToCache`, which simply opens the relevant cache and inserts all the given assets:

```js
export const addFilesToCache = async (
  cacheId,
  assets
```

```
) => {
  const cache = await caches.open(cacheId);
  await cache.addAll(assets);
};
```

To begin testing that, first we need to define a default value for `caches`. In the sample repository, the following code lives in the test suite in `src/lib/service-worker.test.js`, but you could also place it in a Vitest setup file, which would make better sense if you had more than one test suite using the Cache API:

```
global.caches = {
  open: () => {},
  keys: () => {},
  delete: () => {}
};
```

Now let's start off with a `describe` block for the `addFilesToCache` function. All it takes is a call to `vi.spyOn` together with a hand-rolled cache object. Both the `caches` spy and the `cache` stub implement just enough for the purposes of testing the `addFilesToCache` function, nothing more, nothing less:

```
describe('addFilesToCache', () => {
  let cache;

  beforeEach(() => {
    cache = {
      addAll: vi.fn()
    };

    vi.spyOn(global.caches, 'open');
    caches.open.mockResolvedValue(cache);
  });
});
```

Then the tests themselves are straightforward:

```
it('opens the cache with the given id', async () => {
  await addFilesToCache('cache-id', []);
  expect(global.caches.open).toBeCalledWith(
    'cache-id'
  );
});

it('adds all provided assets to the cache', async () => {
  const assets = [1, 2, 3];
```

```
  await addFilesToCache('cache-id', assets);
  expect(cache.addAll).toBeCalledWith(assets);
});
```

Next, here's the definition of deleteOldCaches, which is a bit more complex:

```
export const deleteOldCaches = async (cacheId) => {
  for (const key of await caches.keys()) {
    if (key !== cacheId) await caches.delete(key);
  }
};
```

It turns out that our spy setup for this is much simpler:

```
describe('deleteOldCaches', () => {
  beforeEach(() => {
    vi.spyOn(global.caches, 'keys');
    vi.spyOn(global.caches, 'delete');
  });
```

Then, the tests themselves are fairly straightforward. Notice how each of the tests is self-contained, with their own stub values for the cache.keys function:

```
it('calls keys to retrieve all keys', async () => {
  caches.keys.mockResolvedValue([]);
  await deleteOldCaches('cache-id');
  expect(caches.keys).toBeCalled();
});

it('delete all caches with the provided keys', async () => {
  caches.keys.mockResolvedValue([
    'cache-one',
    'cache-two'
  ]);

  await deleteOldCaches('cache-id');

  expect(caches.delete).toBeCalledWith('cache-one');
  expect(caches.delete).toBeCalledWith('cache-two');
});

it('does not delete the cache with the provided id', async () => {
  caches.keys.mockResolvedValue(['cache-id']);
  await deleteOldCaches('cache-id');
```

```
    expect(caches.delete).not.toBeCalledWith(
      'cache-id'
    );
  });
```

Finally, we come to the `fetchWithCacheOnError` function, the most complex of the three. This involves the Cache API and the Fetch API, so our tests will need to deal with the `request` and `response` objects:

```
export const fetchWithCacheOnError = async (
  cacheId,
  request
) => {
  const cache = await caches.open(cacheId);

  try {
    const response = await fetch(request);

    if (response.status === 200) {
      cache.put(request, response.clone());
    }

    return response;
  } catch {
    return cache.match(request);
  }
};
```

Let's take a look at the test setup. In addition to the `caches.open` spy and the `cache` stub; there's also a `successResponse` object and a `request` object. These have dummy values: calling `successResponse.clone()` doesn't give you back a response, and `request` isn't a real request object. They're just strings. But that's all we need for the tests:

```
describe('fetchWithCacheOnError', () => {
  const successResponse = {
    status: 200,
    clone: () => 'cloned response'
  };
  const request = 'request';

  let cache;

  beforeEach(() => {
    cache = {
```

```
      put: vi.fn(),
      match: vi.fn()
    };

    vi.spyOn(global.caches, 'open');
    caches.open.mockResolvedValue(cache);
    vi.spyOn(global, 'fetch');
    fetch.mockResolvedValue(successResponse);
  });
});
```

Now let's look at the four happy path tests. These tests assume a working network connection and a valid HTTP response with a 200 status code:

```
it('opens the cache with the given id', async () => {
  await fetchWithCacheOnError('cache-id', request);
  expect(global.caches.open).toBeCalledWith(
    'cache-id'
  );
});

it('calls fetch with the request', async () => {
  await fetchWithCacheOnError('cache-id', request);
  expect(global.fetch).toBeCalledWith(request);
});

it('caches the response after cloning', async () => {
  await fetchWithCacheOnError('cache-id', request);
  expect(cache.put).toBeCalledWith(
    request,
    'cloned response'
  );
});

it('returns the response', async () => {
  const result = await fetchWithCacheOnError(
    'cache-id',
    request
  );

  expect(result).toEqual(successResponse);
});
```

Then we have a test for an HTTP status code of anything other than 200:

```
it('does not cache the response if the status code is not 200', async
() => {
  fetch.mockResolvedValue({ status: 404 });
  await fetchWithCacheOnError('cache-id', request);
  expect(cache.put).not.toBeCalled();
});
```

Finally, we have a nested context for the network error. Note the use of mockRejectedValue instead of mockResolvedValue, which will throw an exception and cause the catch block to be executed:

```
describe('when fetch returns a network error', () => {
  let cachedResponse = 'cached-response';

  beforeEach(() => {
    fetch.mockRejectedValue({});
    cache.match.mockResolvedValue(cachedResponse);
  });

  it('retrieve the cached value', async () => {
    await fetchWithCacheOnError(
      'cache-id',
      request
    );

    expect(cache.match).toBeCalledWith(request);
  });

  it('returns the cached value', async () => {
    const result = await fetchWithCacheOnError(
      'cache-id',
      request
    );

    expect(result).toEqual(cachedResponse);
  });
});
```

And that's it: we have a fully-tested service worker using a combination of Playwright and Vitest tests.

Summary

We've finished the book by looking at how even a complex browser feature, such as service workers, can be fully covered by tests.

You've seen how Playwright tests should always test the benefit provided by the implementation – in this case, checking that the page is available offline – rather than testing an implementation detail, such as whether the service worker is is available or not.

You've also seen how the Vitest tests can avoid checking the awkward service worker interface by pushing the majority of the implementation into plain JavaScript functions.

And with that, our tour of test-driven Svelte comes to an end. It's now over to you to put what you've learned into practice.

As this book has shown, there are many avenues that your testing practice can follow. I encourage you to experiment and find what works for you. Seek out the practices that make your life easier and allow you to build higher-quality software at a steady rate.

Thank you for choosing to spend your time with this book. If you have any feedback, good or bad, I'd love to hear it. You can contact me via the book's GitHub repository or via my website at `www.danielirvine.com`.

Index

www.packtpub.com

Subscribe to our online digital library for full access to over 7,000 books and videos, as well as industry leading tools to help you plan your personal development and advance your career. For more information, please visit our website.

Why subscribe?

- Spend less time learning and more time coding with practical eBooks and Videos from over 4,000 industry professionals

- Improve your learning with Skill Plans built especially for you

- Get a free eBook or video every month

- Fully searchable for easy access to vital information

- Copy and paste, print, and bookmark content

Did you know that Packt offers eBook versions of every book published, with PDF and ePub files available? You can upgrade to the eBook version at packtpub.com and as a print book customer, you are entitled to a discount on the eBook copy. Get in touch with us at customercare@packtpub.com for more details.

At www.packtpub.com, you can also read a collection of free technical articles, sign up for a range of free newsletters, and receive exclusive discounts and offers on Packt books and eBooks.

Other Books You May Enjoy

If you enjoyed this book, you may be interested in these other books by Packt:

Mastering React Test-Driven Development

Daniel Irvine

ISBN: 978-1-80324-712-0

- Build test-driven applications using React 18 and Jest
- Understand techniques and patterns for writing great automated tests
- Use test doubles and mocks effectively
- Test-drive browser APIs, including the Fetch API and the WebSocket API
- Integrate with libraries such as React Router, Redux, and Relay (GraphQL)
- Use Cucumber.js and Puppeteer to build Behaviour- Driven Development (BDD) style tests for your applications
- Build and test async Redux code using redux-saga and expect-redux

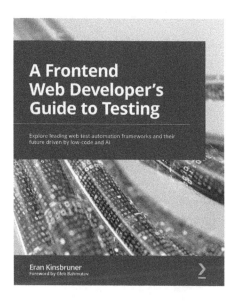

A Frontend Web Developer's Guide to Testing

Eran Kinsbruner

ISBN: 978-1-80323-831-9

- Choose the ideal tool or combination of tools for testing your app
- Continuously monitor the market and ensure that your developers are using the right tools
- Advance test automation for your web app with sophisticated capabilities
- Measure both code coverage and test coverage to assess your web application quality
- Measure the success and maturity of web application quality
- Understand the trade-offs in tool selection and the associated risks
- Build Cypress, Selenium, Playwright, and Puppeteer projects from scratch
- Explore low-code testing tools for web apps

Packt is searching for authors like you

If you're interested in becoming an author for Packt, please visit `authors.packtpub.com` and apply today. We have worked with thousands of developers and tech professionals, just like you, to help them share their insight with the global tech community. You can make a general application, apply for a specific hot topic that we are recruiting an author for, or submit your own idea.

Share Your Thoughts

Now you've finished *Svelte with Test-Driven Development*, we'd love to hear your thoughts! Scan the QR code below to go straight to the Amazon review page for this book and share your feedback or leave a review on the site that you purchased it from.

`https://www.amazon.in/review/create-review/error?asin=1837638330`

Your review is important to us and the tech community and will help us make sure we're delivering excellent quality content.

Download a free PDF copy of this book

Thanks for purchasing this book!

Do you like to read on the go but are unable to carry your print books everywhere?

Is your eBook purchase not compatible with the device of your choice?

Don't worry, now with every Packt book you get a DRM-free PDF version of that book at no cost.

Read anywhere, any place, on any device. Search, copy, and paste code from your favorite technical books directly into your application.

The perks don't stop there, you can get exclusive access to discounts, newsletters, and great free content in your inbox daily

Follow these simple steps to get the benefits:

1. Scan the QR code or visit the link below

https://packt.link/free-ebook/9781837638338

2. Submit your proof of purchase
3. That's it! We'll send your free PDF and other benefits to your email directly

Ingram Content Group UK Ltd.
Milton Keynes UK
UKHW030709190723
425405UK00008B/201